THE TROPICAL AGRICUL

General Editor, Livestock Volumes
Anthony J. Smith

Beef

David Richardson
Rangeland Modelling Group
Department of Mathematics and Applied Mathematics
University of Cape Town, South Africa

Anthony J. Smith
Tropical Agriculture Association
Scotland

partageons les connaissances au profit des communautés rurales

sharing knowledge, improving rural livelihoods

Macmillan Education
Between Towns Road, Oxford OX4 3PP
A division of Macmillan Publishers Limited
Companies and representatives throughout the world

www.macmillan-africa.com
www.macmillan-caribbean.com

Published in co-operation with the ACP–EU Technical Centre for Agricultural
and Rural Cooperation (CTA), Postbus 380, 6700 AJ Wageningen,
The Netherlands

ISBN-13: 978-0-333-59833-7
ISBN-10: 0-333-59833-4

Editing and layout: Green Ink Ltd, UK

Cover design: Jim Weaver Design

Cover photograph: Zebu cattle in Western Kenya (Sue Parrott, Green Ink)

All photographs are reproduced by courtesy of the authors except the
following: Figs 32 and 33 by N. Pullen; Fig 36 by R. Matthewman; Fig 49 by
C. Daborn.

Printed and bound in Malaysia

2010   2009   2008   2007   2006
10 9   8   7   6   5   4   3   2

CTA

partageons les connaissances au profit des communautés rurales

sharing knowledge, improving rural livelihoods

The Technical Centre for Agricultural and Rural Cooperation (CTA) was established in 1983 under the Lomé Convention between the ACP (African, Caribbean and Pacific) Group of States and the European Union Member States. Since 2000, it has operated within the framework of the ACP–EC Cotonou Agreement.

CTA's tasks are to develop and provide services that improve access to information for agricultural and rural development, and to strengthen the capacity of ACP countries to produce, acquire, exchange and utilise information in this area. CTA's programmes are designed to: provide a wide range of information products and services and enhance awareness of relevant information sources; promote the integrated use of appropriate communication channels and intensify contacts and information exchange (particularly intra-ACP); and develop ACP capacity to generate and manage agricultural information and to formulate information and communication management strategies, including those relevant to science and technology. CTA's work incorporates new developments in methodologies and cross-cutting issues such as gender and social capital.

CTA, Postbus 380, 6700 AJ Wageningen, The Netherlands.

Contents

Preface

Beef production in developed countries has changed substantially during the past 50 years. Historically, beef was produced extensively from specialised beef herds, but nowadays beef is also produced as a by-product from dairy herds and from herds kept intensively and fed on high-energy diets.

In developing countries, there is little intensive production and specialist beef herds are uncommon (except for parts of South America and a few African countries). In traditional livestock systems, meat may not be the most important product, while survival of the animals is more important than rapid growth or weight gain. However, large numbers of cattle are kept in the tropics, where they provide the main livelihood for the people who manage them.

This book complements the volume entitled *Dairying* in this series and addresses the needs of the traditional cattle keeper (smallholders and pastoralists) and the cattle rancher or businessman practising more intensive or western-type systems of beef production. Development workers, non-governmental organisations (NGOs) and extension workers will also find this book useful. Written by specialists who have spent many years working in tropical countries, it concentrates on the production of meat from cattle but also deals with cattle production systems in their entirety. We summarise the information on beef production that is relevant to the tropics and that is widely scattered in the literature. Some of the sources that have been particularly useful are listed at the end of the book.

Anthony Smith, May 2005

1 Introduction

Distribution of beef cattle

Beef is defined as meat derived from cattle or buffaloes. The meat of young milk-fed calves is usually known as veal, but veal is considered to be a luxury product and is not normally produced in developing countries. Beef is produced wherever cattle are kept, unless there are religious prohibitions against the slaughter and eating of cattle. Because domestic cattle are found in almost all the countries of the world between the Arctic and Antarctic circles and because almost all cattle are eventually slaughtered for food, beef production is a worldwide activity. However, the methods of production are as varied as the producers and their environments.

Of the world's 1358 million cattle, 76 per cent are found in developing and 24 per cent in developed countries. However, since beef yields in developed countries are higher, the amount of beef produced is similar (see Table 1). The highest figure for output of beef per animal is achieved by the United States. Production figures for many African countries are low but may not reflect the real output, since only beef marketed through formal channels is recorded. Substantial amounts of meat consumed by farming and pastoral communities may be excluded from the national statistics; for example in KwaZulu in South Africa, more cattle are slaughtered informally than are sold or slaughtered through the formal system. However, even after allowing for these factors, beef production in most developing countries is extremely low.

The availability of beef tends to increase with standard of living and is very high in the United States; it is also fairly high in South America. Beef availability in sub-Saharan Africa is generally low, but figures may be misleading since informal slaughter is seldom recorded by official statistics. In most developing countries the consumption of beef by the wealthiest section of the population is similar to that in western countries, while the poor consume much less than the national average.

1

Table 1 Cattle population, national beef production and yield of beef in selected regions and countries

Country or region	Cattle population (millions)	Total beef production (1000 t)	Human population (millions)	Beef yield (kg/person /annum)	Beef yield (kg/animal /annum)
World	1358.0	58742.0	6134.0	9.6	43.3
Developing countries	1034.0	29721.0	4816.0	6.2	28.7
Developed countries	324.0	29514.0	1318.0	22.4	91.1
USA	96.7	12438.0	285.0	43.6	128.6
EU	80.7	7530.0	377.0	20.0	93.3
LAC	362.0	14463.0	526.0	27.5	40.0
Jamaica	0.4	13.0	2.5	5.2	32.5
Cuba	4.0	77.0	11.2	6.9	19.3
Brazil	176.0	7136.0	172.0	41.5	40.6
SSA	214.0	2936.0	623.0	4.7	13.7
Chad	5.9	73.0	8.0	9.1	12.4
Botswana	1.7	32.0	1.5	21.3	18.8
Ethiopia	35.5	304.0	64.0	4.8	8.6
Kenya	13.5	295.0	31.0	9.5	21.9
Nigeria	20.0	376.0	117.0	3.2	18.8
Senegal	3.2	5.0	10.0	0.5	1.6
S. Africa	13.7	579.0	44.0	13.2	42.3
Zimbabwe	5.7	101.0	13.0	7.8	17.7
Asia	474.0	14145.0	3720.0	3.8	29.8

EU = European Union; LAC = Latin America and Caribbean;
SSA = Sub-Saharan Africa
Source: FAO (2004)

Annual rainfall markedly affects the type of livestock produced and in very dry areas (< 200 mm), stockowners seldom keep cattle. Cattle can survive in areas where rainfall is above 200 mm per annum. Where annual rainfall is between 200 and 600 mm, livestock production systems are usually pastoralist or nomadic. Above 600 mm, mixed crop–livestock systems are the norm (Table 2).

In Africa, the area suitable for beef production is limited by the threat of tsetse-borne trypanosomiasis (Fig 1). The disease occurs in relatively high rainfall (> 500 mm per annum) zones (see Chapter 2).

In many parts of Africa, the Caribbean and the Pacific, cattle fulfil a range of different functions, including production of meat and milk, the store of wealth and provision of draught power. Cattle will more often be slaughtered for home use than produced with the beef market in mind.

Table 2 Relationship between animal production and rainfall in the tropics

Annual rainfall	Type of livestock production	Animals kept
50–200 mm	Pastoralist herds and flocks move over large distances	Camels, fat-tailed sheep, goats
200–500 mm	Pastoralist	Cattle, goats, sheep
500–1000 mm	Pastoralist and sedentary occupation of land not used for crop production	Cattle, goats, sheep, poultry
> 1000 mm	Sedentary animal production often closely linked to crop production	Cattle, goats, sheep, poultry, pigs

Source: adapted from Pagot (1985)

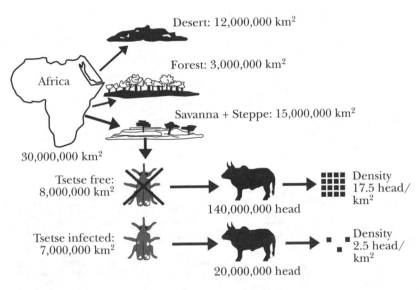

Fig 1 *Areas affected by tsetse-borne trypanosomiasis (Jasiorowski, 1976)*

In southern Africa, over 80 per cent of small-scale cattle owners cite milk production as an important reason for keeping cattle (Schmidt, 1990). Cattle in Africa fulfil an important role in storing wealth since they yield a better return on capital than short-term savings accounts or fixed deposits. This holds true despite the low calving rates (40–50 per cent per annum) and high mortality (8–10 per cent) that are common in traditional production systems. Furthermore, cash may be realised almost immediately by selling the animals; this is not possible with high interest bank accounts. The value of cattle also keeps up with the rate of inflation.

3

In many parts of the tropics, both oxen and cows are used for draught power (although in some countries, such as India and Nepal, cows are not traditionally used for work). Working cattle are especially important in high rainfall areas, where crop production may be dependent on animal traction (Fig 2). In mixed crop–livestock systems, cattle consume forage and crop residues that are of no food value to man. They also provide manure, which can be added to the soil to improve its structure and fertility.

The scope of the book

In developed countries, beef production has increased substantially during the past 50 years due to increasingly intensive methods of production and to changes in the genotypes of cattle. Beef production from commercial rangeland in the tropical regions of Australia and Africa has also increased. However, when commenting on animal production in the developing areas of Africa, Blair-Rains and Kassim (1979) observed that 'half a century of animal disease prevention and eradication measures, several decades of grassland and pasture investigations and research into most aspects of animal nutrition and genetics have scarcely affected animal production'. This apparent lack of success is due partly to the failure of development agencies and planners to consider the multi-purpose role of small-scale herds and the specific needs of their owners.

Fig 2 *Cattle preparing land for crops in Ethiopia*

4

Furthermore, the effects of variable rainfall and the spatial heterogeneity of rangeland on small-scale cattle owners have been largely ignored.

This book attempts to provide the knowledge required to understand the workings of cattle production systems in the tropics. It deals with technical issues faced by commercial producers of high quality beef and small-scale keepers of multi-purpose herds, where beef is only one of the products required. Beef production is examined within the context of the environment, the needs of the cattle owners and the potential of the animals. The reader is encouraged to consider the implications of any management changes on the productivity of the system as a whole. The idea is put forward that development of beef production in the tropics is likely to be achieved by small incremental changes.

The tropics officially span the area between the Tropic of Cancer at latitude 23° 28' North and the Tropic of Capricorn at the same latitude South. However, since the true tropics and the transitional areas to the north and south are similar in many ways, the area considered in this book is within 30° north and south of the equator.

2 Producing beef in a tropical environment

Effects of climate

The climate of a tropical or sub-tropical country can be arid (little or no rainfall), semi-arid (hot with little cloud cover, low humidity and a short rainy season) or hot, humid and cloudy with rainfall throughout the year. In highland regions the climate may be cooler, sometimes resembling temperate conditions. It is important to understand the effects of climate on cattle production because most research has been carried out in temperate regions, where the high-producing breeds were developed. Considerable modifications to the environment must be made if such breeds are to produce effectively in the tropics. The adverse effects of high ambient temperatures can be reduced by management strategies, including providing adequate water and shade and modifying feeding regimes (e.g. allowing cattle to graze at night).

The effects of climate can be direct (i.e. temperature, solar radiation, day length, humidity, rainfall and wind) and indirect (i.e. availability of forage and water, incidence of disease and parasites). The amount and composition of forage available to cattle is affected by the long-term mean annual rainfall, the yearly variation in rainfall and the soil type. The climate also influences the availability of surplus grain, crop residues and by-products; the incidence of parasites and diseases; and the consumption of poisonous plants.

Ambient temperature and solar radiation

When considering the effects of ambient temperature on cattle, it is important to take account of seasonal and diurnal (daily) differences that occur throughout the year as well as the mean annual temperature. For example, in coastal and low-lying parts of the humid tropics, the mean monthly temperature range is only 2–3°C, whilst in arid or desert areas the mean monthly temperature may range from 17 to 45°C. Diurnal temperature ranges can be equally great. Cattle in the semi-arid tropics may experience cool temperatures at night, which allow a period of recovery from the stress of high daytime temperatures; but in the humid tropics, night temperatures are similar to those of the day. Mean annual temperature therefore cannot be used as a satisfactory index for assessing the suitability of an area for a given type of cattle.

Exposure to cold ambient temperatures is not normally regarded as a factor adversely affecting cattle production in the tropics. However, at high altitudes in the dry season, temperatures can fall below 0°C at night. When very young calves consuming very small quantities of milk are subject to such low temperatures, the metabolic heat produced is less than the heat loss from the body, and body reserves must be catabolised to provide energy to prevent a drop in body temperature. This could lead to slow or negative growth rates and an increase in mortality.

Ultraviolet light causes sunburn in white cattle that have a white skin. Many tropical cattle have a black skin underneath a white coat and are therefore less affected. Ultraviolet light can cause epithelioma in the unpigmented eyes of white-faced Herefords. The effect of solar radiation on the body temperature of cattle may be best understood in terms of the heat balance of the animal as it tries to maintain constant body temperature:

Heat balance = solar radiation + metabolic heat
− evaporative heat loss − other heat losses

When animals are exposed to sunlight in the tropics, solar radiation may contribute 70 per cent of the total heat load, while metabolic heat contributes only about 30 per cent (Table 3). Heat loss by convection is small; most heat is lost from the animal by re-radiation and evaporation of water (mainly sweating and respiration). If absorbed solar radiation and metabolic heat production together exceed the evaporative and other heat losses, then heat is stored and body temperature will rise. Cattle adapt to this situation in several ways. They may reduce the heat load acquired from solar radiation by grazing and travelling at night or when the elevation of the sun is low and by seeking shade during the hottest part of the day (Fig 3). They may orientate themselves to the sun in a way that minimises their absorption of solar radiation. Unlike camels, which have a very labile body temperature, they need to maintain their body temperature close to 39°C.

If the body temperature rises above 39°C, cattle will raise their respiratory rate and sweat to increase evaporative heat loss. Zebu cattle can do this more effectively than taurine (European) breeds because they have more effective sweat glands. Long-term exposure to hot conditions can lead to a reduction in the voluntary intake of feed by cattle. This reduces the production of metabolic heat and the amount of heat that must be lost (see *Livestock Behaviour, Management and Welfare* in this series). The

7

Table 3   Heat balance of _Bos indicus_ at noon

	kcal/m²/hour
Metabolic heat production	59
Radiant heat absorbed[1]	742
Re-radiated heat	462
Convective heat loss	74
Cutaneous heat loss	170
Respiratory heat loss	42
Heat storage[2]	9
Gain	801
Loss	757

1 The amount of energy gained from the environment is about 12 times that produced from the animal's internal metabolism
2 The animal is storing 9 kcal/m²/hour and therefore its body temperature is rising
Source: adapted from Robertshaw and Finch (1976)

reported reductions in milk yields and growth rates of animals subjected to high temperatures are largely a reflection of the reduction in metabolisable energy intake and to a lesser extent an effect of heat on the productive processes. The amount of heat produced increases soon after animals are fed. Therefore feeding them the bulk of their ration in the evening can be a good strategy in the semi-arid tropics. A decrease in ambient temperature, an increase in wind speed and a wet coat due to rain will increase the rate of heat loss.

During a drought, intense solar radiation and dehydration due to scarcity of drinking water encourage cattle to rest. However, prolonged

Fig 3   _Mashona bull seeking shade (Zimbabwe)_

grazing times are needed to enable animals to obtain adequate feed from sparse pastures. These factors contribute to the weight loss that commonly occurs during periods of drought.

Humidity and wind

The effect of humidity on livestock will depend on the extent to which evaporation from the body surface forms part of the heat-regulating mechanisms. Humans rely more on evaporative cooling because they can sweat much more than cattle and therefore the humidity of the air at high ambient temperatures has a greater effect on man than on cattle. High atmospheric humidity reduces the rate of evaporation and heat loss; consequently, cattle body temperatures will rise at a lower air temperature under humid conditions than when the air is dry.

Air movement tends to be greater in hot, dry areas than in hot, humid areas. Air movement encourages evaporation and causes additional cooling, leading to 'wind chill'. Locating cattle accommodation to take advantage of cooling breezes is therefore an advantage in hot areas, while young calves should be protected from draughts in cool areas.

Long-term rainfall and rainfall variability

Table 2 (page 3) summarises how long-term annual rainfall influences vegetation type and cattle production system. Variability in annual rainfall increases as mean annual rainfall decreases. In regions of less than 1000 mm mean annual rainfall, where cattle are largely dependent on rangeland, the difference between years in annual rainfall is substantial. This leads to a wide variation in herbage production. In areas of variable rainfall, there is much more forage available during the rainy season. If large weight losses are to be avoided during the dry season, stockowners need to find ways of conserving forage (e.g. as standing hay, silage or straw). Two processes influence herbage composition. First, as the plant matures, the proportions of leaf and protein decrease, while the proportions of fibre and stem increase. Second, selective grazing by cattle removes leaf in preference to stem, thereby exacerbating the decline in protein content of the available herbage. Further information on this subject can be found in *Forage Husbandry* and *Ruminant Nutrition* in this series.

Soil type

During years of low rainfall, the infiltration rate of rain into clay soils is lower than that into coarse-grained sandy soils. As herbage growth is directly related to soil moisture, more herbage is therefore produced per hectare by sandy soils than by heavy clay soils. However, clay soils are more fertile than sandy ones, so when rainfall and available moisture are adequate, the herbage yield will be greater on clay soils.

Availability of surplus grain, crop residues and by-products

In the tropics, production of grain surplus to human requirements is feasible only in regions where the mean annual rainfall exceeds 600 mm. Many developing countries do not produce surplus grain and cattle are fed on crop residues and by-products when there is insufficient pasture. Crop residues such as straw, stover, husks and chaff are usually available in crop-growing regions. In marginal areas, the whole drought-damaged crop may be offered to cattle during years of low rainfall. A detailed discussion of the use of residues can be found in *Forage Husbandry* in this series.

Incidence of parasites and diseases

High ambient temperatures and high humidity favour the multiplication of external and internal parasites. External parasites are vectors of major diseases such as anaplasmosis, babesiosis (redwater), heartwater and theileriosis. Heavy tick burdens can cause toxicosis and anaemia, which adversely affect productivity. Streptothricosis (or dermatophilosis) is a serious disease that occurs in the humid tropics of Africa. Some indigenous cattle (e.g. the N'Dama) are tolerant to the disease but exotic and some indigenous cattle are not (Fig 4). For detailed coverage of these diseases see the two *Animal Health* volumes in this series.

In Africa, between 68 and 90 per cent of the tropical rain forest and forest zones are infested by tsetse flies, which transmit trypanosomiasis. This is the greatest single obstacle to cattle production in these areas.

Fig 4   Bos indicus *suffering from extreme infection with streptothricosis (W. Africa)*

Some breeds indigenous to these regions, such as the N'Dama, are trypanotolerant and are able to survive in tsetse-infested areas. However, trypanotolerant cattle may succumb to the disease when lactating or when used for work. Trypanosome infection leads to decreases in milk yield and calf growth. Semi-arid and arid regions are virtually free from tsetse flies and tsetse-borne trypanosomiasis.

Poisonous plants

Several hundred species of tropical plants are potentially poisonous to cattle, but cattle tend to avoid most of them and will normally consume them only when pastures are overgrazed or when the poisonous plants are contained within conserved fodder. Some toxic plants sprout early in the season and may be consumed before the grass grows. Poisoning can be prevented by avoiding such areas until the grass is plentiful. Exotic animals may consume poisonous plants when introduced to a new area, while indigenous livestock avoid them. For example, umkausan (*Dichapetalum cymosum*) occurs in the drier parts of Zimbabwe and is only eaten by cattle at the end of the dry season. The cattle die when they drink water after eating this plant.

Some crop residues can be toxic, for example wilted sorghum plants can cause prussic acid poisoning. Most traditional cattle keepers know which plants to avoid and have strategies to prevent poisoning.

Systems of production

Specialist beef herds and beef from the dairy industry

Specialist beef production systems aim to achieve the optimum output for a specific environment. Producers try to maximise the quality and unit value of the beef produced by maturing and marketing animals as young as possible. Genotypes and body weight at slaughter are selected to ensure optimum fleshing without excess fat. Specialist commercial beef units are common in developed countries but not found in large numbers in Africa, the Caribbean or the Pacific. However, they do occur in areas where there is a market for high quality beef, such as parts of southern Africa.

In Europe, the dairy industry supplies a high proportion of the beef and veal consumed. Even in the United Kingdom, which has a tradition of specialised beef herds and where many beef breeds of international importance were developed, 65 per cent of the beef consumed originates from dairy herds: from bull calves and from cull cows at the end of their productive lives. Dairy calves may be economically reared for beef if

11

surplus whole milk, skimmed milk or milk substitutes are available at a reasonable price or if cereal concentrates are plentiful and cheap. This system of production is uneconomic in most parts of Africa, the Caribbean and the Pacific.

Smallholder production systems

Small-scale cattle owners in developing countries tend to keep multipurpose herds. They use their cattle to provide milk and draught power, and beef is a product obtained only at the end of the animal's productive life. The animals are often kept as part of a mixed crop–livestock system where they can be fed on crop by-products (e.g. maize stover) during the dry season. Some are stall-fed with harvested forage such as Napier grass, planted by the smallholder.

These types of systems should aim to produce the optimum amount of meat that is compatible with the other functions of the animals. However, many animals offered for sale or slaughter are in too poor a condition to produce meat of adequate quality for commercial markets. Furthermore, many of these animals may be condemned at formal abattoirs as unfit for human consumption because they are too thin. This is a waste because, if feed is available, they can be fattened to an acceptable standard in only a short period of time. With limited inputs of concentrates and plentiful supplies of roughage, mature draught oxen and dry cull cows gain bodyweight and condition rapidly. This leads to a substantial increase in the weight of edible meat in the carcass. In Zimbabwe, until the mid-1980s, the Cold Storage Commission (a parastatal abattoir company) provided feedlots for fattening cattle prior to slaughter and the cost was deducted from the payment made to the farmer for the carcass. Many cattle from subsistence communities were fattened in this way.

Pastoralist systems

In tropical areas where annual rainfall is less than 400 mm, it is too dry to grow crops and here, livestock provide the only viable form of livelihood. Beef is one of a range of different outputs produced by pastoralists such as the Fulani in West Africa (Fig 5) and the Maasai in East Africa. These communities keep cattle mainly for milk. They sometimes take blood from their cattle, but animals are slaughtered for meat generally only on ceremonial occasions. When meat is required for the family, it is usually obtained from the sheep and goats that are kept alongside the cattle. This is partly because a sheep or goat carcass can be eaten by a small number of people while it is still fresh. Another reason is that sheep and goats reproduce much faster than cattle. Goats can increase their numbers by 45 percent each year and sheep by 25 per cent, whereas cattle

Fig 5   *Fulani cattle on the Jos Plateau in Nigeria*

numbers can increase by only 10 per cent. Pastoralist cattle are regarded as a type of 'bank', since they can be sold for cash in times of hardship, such as drought, and to meet family needs, such as school fees or health care. Pastoralist herds are often kept on common ground. They are regarded as symbols of status and wealth in the community and, traditionally, numbers are more important than the condition of the individuals.

Many rangeland areas are prone to episodes of severe drought, when large numbers of animals may die. The type of cattle kept in pastoralist systems therefore need to be hardy and adapted to such conditions. It is difficult to measure just how much land is required to maintain a herd because animals are moved from area to area. For example, the Fulani move their cattle south during the dry season to areas where the grazing is better and where crop residues provide additional fodder. They move north during the rainy season to avoid the risk of tsetse-borne trypanosomiasis. The number of animals that can be managed during the dry season may be limited by the availability of labour to water the herd. Each cow, steer or bull requires 40 litres of water per day. Fig 6 provides an example from Ethiopia and illustrates the high labour demands of watering the herd from a deep well, especially when only basic equipment is available.

Herd size and composition

The maximum natural fertility of cattle is one calf per cow per annum, although in practice this is rarely achieved. Reproduction rates tend to be higher in intensive systems than on extensive rangeland. Beef cattle

13

Fig 6 *Watering cattle in Ethiopia*

are not normally slaughtered before 15 months of age in intensive systems
and at 2.5 to 4.5 years in extensive rangeland systems. Cull cows and
draught animals may be 11 years or older when they are slaughtered.

Although a degree of stratification exists within the cattle industries of
some developing countries, whereby young animals are reared to weaning or older on one farm or communal grazing area and finished in
another area, most cattle in the tropics are raised from birth to slaughter
on the same land. Stockowners therefore need to know how many
breeding cows and progeny they can keep on their land. Herd composition calculations are also important for working out the feed requirements of intensive herds.

The carrying capacity of rangeland is defined by the Food and Agriculture Organization of the United Nations (FAO) (Pratt, 2005) as the
maximum number of herbivores that can be supported on a sustainable
basis, based on a daily dry matter (DM) intake of 2.5–3.0 per cent of their
live weight. It is usually expressed in Livestock Units (LSU). Animals are
rated according to the relative amounts of herbage that they will consume. One LSU is defined as a 500 kg bovine. Thus one LSU will require
5.0–5.4 tonnes of dry feed per year. However, only 30–45 per cent of
herbage is available to cattle since up to 30 per cent is trampled,
consumed by insects or decomposes, and cattle cannot graze on very short
grass. Furthermore, excessive defoliation of herbage in one year is likely
to reduce availability in subsequent years. Thus, the amount of forage
required is between 10.2 and 18 tonnes per LSU per annum. In the Sahel,
DM production is 0.615, 1.1 and 1.7 tonnes/ha along the 200, 400 and
600 mm isohyets (lines of equal rainfall) respectively. The figures indicate

that the carrying capacity of the rangeland increases from 0.055 to 0.166 LSU/ha as the rainfall increases.

The LSU values for animals of different sizes and the method of calculating herd LSU are shown in Table 4. In this example, the total herd is equivalent to 206 LSU. If the available grazing is 4000 ha and has a carrying capacity of 0.125 LSU/ha, the area will be able to carry 0.125 x 4000 = 500 LSU. The numbers of animals in each class should be multiplied by 500/206 = 2.43 to give the appropriate herd composition. Thus, the herd would contain 194 breeding cows, 49 cull cows, 49 replacement heifers, and so on.

In parts of the tropics where cattle are very small even at maturity, the Tropical Livestock Unit (TLU) is used instead of the LSU. One TLU is equivalent to an animal with a body mass of 250 kg. The method of calculation is similar to that described for LSU.

Calving rate and mortality vary with the standard of management. The owner's objectives may also play a role, for example, calf mortality may be high in some multi-purpose herds, where milk production for human use is more important than rearing calves for beef. High calf mortality will affect herd composition, since it will cause an increase in the proportion of mature females.

Commercial and small-scale producers approach the subjects of herd size and herd composition from different perspectives. The size of a commercial herd is determined by the total number of LSU that may be carried in accordance with the recommended capacity of the range. The

Table 4   Livestock units and herd composition per 100 breeding cows

Class	Body wt (kg)	LSU value	Number	Total LSU
Breeding cows (mated)	450	0.90	80	72.0
Cows to be culled	450	0.90	20	18.0
Calves	150	0.30	60	18.0
Breeding heifers (replacements)	360	0.72	20	14.4
Steers, 1.5 yrs	275	0.55	27	14.9
Heifers, 1.5 yrs	260	0.52	27	14.0
Steers, 2.5 yrs	375	0.75	26	19.5
Cull heifers, 2.5 yrs	360	0.72	6	4.3
Steers, 3.5 yrs	475	0.95	25	23.8
Bulls[1]	700	1.40	5	7.0
Total			296	205.9

The assumptions made are as follows: calving rate 60%; mortality of 10% for calves and 3% for older stock; cow replacement rate of 20% per year
1 Bulls comprise 4% of breeding females mated plus 10% spares

system of production chosen by the producer will influence the age at which animals are sold or slaughtered (the percentage of a herd that is slaughtered on the farm or sold is known as 'off-take'). Calving rate, mortality and age at sale or slaughter determine the numbers of each class and age group that make up the herd composition (see Table 5).

At constant LSU, the number of cows in the herd decreases as the calving rate increases. At the same time, the total number of animals increases because there is an increase in the proportion of calves and yearlings, which make a smaller contribution to the total LSU. The percentage off-take increases with an increase in the calving rate, with a decrease in mortality and with a reduction in the age at slaughter. These changes also lead to an increase in the proportion of young, high quality steers and heifers among the animals sold. At the same time, a reduction in the age of steers marketed results in an increase in the number of breeding cows in a herd of constant LSU. However, marketing slaughter cattle at 1.5 years or younger requires large amounts of grain or application of large amounts of fertilizer to planted pastures. In a herd with a

Table 5 Herd composition and off-take per 1,000 LSU per year for different weaning and mortality rates and age of progeny when sold (commercial herd)

Calving rate (%)	50	50	70	90	90
Age at sale (years)	3.5	3.5	3.5	3.5	1.5
Mortality					
Calves (%)	25	4	4	4	4
Older cattle (%)	4	1	1	1	1
Nos of each class of stock					
Breeding cows	453	396	327	278	411
Breeding heifers	100	99	82	70	103
Cull cows	99	99	82	70	103
Bulls	24	22	18	15	23
Calves	277	247	286	313	463
Steers, 1.5 yrs	104	119	137	150	222
Heifers, 1.5 yrs	104	119	137	150	222
Steers, 2.5 yrs	100	118	136	149	–
Cull heifers, 2.5 yrs	–	19	54	79	–
Steers, 3.5 yrs	96	116	135	147	–
Total head	1357	1354	1394	1421	1547
Off-take					
Steers	96	116	135	147	222
Heifers	–	19	54	79	119
Cull cows	99	99	82	70	103
Total off-take	195	234	271	296	444
Off-take as % of herd	14.4	17.3	19.4	20.8	28.7

calving rate of only 50 per cent and 25 per cent calf mortality, all the two-year-old heifers have to be kept and there is no scope for selecting superior heifers as replacements. In addition, the numbers of aged cull cows and steers sold are similar.

The composition of small-scale herds in developing countries (see Table 6) is often very different from even the least productive system shown in Table 4. Small-scale herds have a higher proportion of cows (for milk, the main product) and mature oxen (for draught power). Sale and slaughter rates tend to be very low and slaughter of a large proportion of oxen at five years of age or older is inevitable when animals are used to provide draught power. The low productivity of communal herds is due largely to low calving rates and high calf mortality, although these figures may vary significantly from year to year.

Table 6 Herd composition and productivity on common land in southern and West Africa

	South Africa[1]	S. Zimbabwe[2]	Central Mali[3]
Herd composition (%)			
Cows	35.6	27.0	33.0
Calves	10.6	13.8	17.0
Heifers and steers (1–3 yrs)	41.4	34.6	30.0
Oxen and bulls	12.4	24.6[4]	20.0
Production factors (%)			
Calving rate	41.1	68.0	
Calf mortality	23.5	24.8	
Herd mortality	13.1	3.8	
Off-take	5.9	9.9	

1 Ciskei and Transkei regions (Bembridge and Tapson, 1993)
2 Scoones (1993)
3 Pagot (1985)
4 The high proportion of mature oxen and bulls in Zimbabwe probably reflects the importance of animal draught power

Table 7 examines the effects of calving rate and percentage off-take on herd size and composition for a village herd of 100 cows grazing on common land. Mortalities of different age classes are assumed to be the same in all herds. The total number of animals sold is largely determined by calving rate. At constant off-take an increase in calving rate is accompanied by an increase in herd size. An increase in off-take leads to a reduction in the age at sale or slaughter and a reduction in the total number of animals and total LSU. The marginal increase in the numbers

Table 7   Herd size and composition in relation to calving rate and off-take for a herd of 100 breeding females

| Calving rate (%) | | 50 | 50 | 90 | 90 |
| Off-take (%) | | 12.2 | 17.5 | 17.7 | 25 |
Age and sex	**LSU**	**Herd composition (nos of animals)**			
Breeding cows	0.90	80	80	80	80
Breeding heifers	0.72	20	20	20	20
Cull cows	0.90	20	20	20	20
Bulls	1.40	5	5	5	5
Calves	0.30	50	50	90	90
Steers, 1.5yrs	0.55	24	24	43	43
Heifers, 1.5yrs	0.52	24	24	43	43
Steers, 2.5yrs	0.75	24	24	43	43
Cull heifers, 2.5yrs	0.72	4	4	23	23
Steers, 3.5yrs	0.95	23	24	42	20
Cull heifers, 3.5yrs	0.90	4			
Steers, 4.5yrs	0.97	23		42	
Cull heifers, 4.5yrs	0.90	1			
Steers, 5.5yrs	1.00	22		29	
Steers, 6.5yrs	1.00	22			
Steers, 7.5yrs	1.00	22			
Total head		368	275	480	387
Total LSU		288	196	343	216
Off-take					
Steers		22(7.5)	24(3.5)	13(4.5)	23(1.5)
Steers			29(5.5)	20(2.5)	
Cull heifers		3(3.5)	4(2.5)	23(2.5)	23(2.5)
Cull cows		20	20	20	20
Total off-take		45	48	85	86

Calf mortality is assumed to be 4% and that of older cattle 1% per annum
Age of animal at sale or slaughter given in brackets
Recommended ratio of bulls to cows is 4 per 100 plus 1 spare

sold is due to the reduction in total mortality as age at disposal increases. A very high off-take (> 25 per cent) precludes the use of steers as draught animals, even if the calving rate is as high as 90 per cent, since they must all be sold or slaughtered at between 1.5 and 2.5 years of age. Systems that retain steers until they are four years or older may be more flexible, since in low-rainfall years, large numbers of non-breeding animals may be sold and few, if any, breeding cows (apart from culls) need to be sold to adjust herd numbers to available grazing.

3 Nutrition

Most stockowners in the tropics have little control over what or how much an animal eats. In the rainy season, adequate feed and water are generally available but in the dry season, the cattle owner may need to find alternatives. Poor quality forage should be supplemented with urea, minerals and vitamins. Beef cattle normally lose weight during the dry season and their management should be geared towards controlling this loss, so the cattle can use the first flush of grass in the rainy season for production rather than for replacing body tissues.

Principles of nutrition

The principles of cattle nutrition are discussed in detail in *Ruminant Nutrition* in this series. This chapter is concerned with understanding how the diet of beef cattle influences their ability to grow, reproduce and rear calves. The science of nutrition is concerned with either predicting the performance of animals given known amounts of specific feeds, or supplying the amounts of nutrients required to sustain a chosen level of production at as low a cost as possible. Four facets of nutrition must be considered:

1. The diet selected by grazing animals or supplied by stockowners.
2. The amount eaten (voluntary intake).
3. The proportion of dietary nutrients broken down, absorbed and available for the animal's metabolic processes (metabolisability, Q).
4. The efficiency of use of absorbed/digested nutrients for productive purposes.

Water

Water is essential for all life and all livestock should be allowed to drink as much water as they wish if maximum productivity is to be achieved.

Depriving beef cattle of water will reduce their intake of feed and so reduce production. (The effects of drought are discussed in Chapter 9.) All feeds contain some water and their composition is usually expressed as dry matter (DM). Ruminants consume 2–4 kg of water per kg of dry matter. This can be ingested as drinking water or contained within the feed itself. Young herbage contains up to 80 per cent water, while hay contains only 10 per cent, so cattle fed on dry feed (e.g. hay) need more drinking water than those kept on fresh pasture.

Energy

Energy drives all living processes and animal production involves converting feed energy into maintenance of the animal and the formation of products such as meat and milk. During growth, energy is stored as protein and fat. In nutrition, energy is measured as megajoules (MJ). Not all the energy in the feed (gross energy or GE) is available to the animal; some is lost in the faeces, some in the urine, and some as the combustible gas methane, which is produced during fermentation in the rumen. The energy available to the animal is known as metabolisable energy (ME). The productivity of an animal is a function of both the amount of feed eaten and the metabolisability (Q) of dietary energy.

Digestible energy (DE) = gross energy – faecal energy

Metabolisable energy (ME) = gross energy – faecal energy – urine energy – methane energy

Q (Metabolisability) = ME/GE

For example, as the amount of feed eaten increases, weight losses decrease or gains increase (Fig 7). The response to an extra kilogram of feed is larger for feeds with 11.3 than those with 7.8 MJ/kg DM (Q = 0.65 vs 0.45). This is largely because more of the feed energy is available to the animal. However, at the same ME intake, the animal eating the feed with the highest ME concentration will gain the most weight because the ME will be used most efficiently, especially if the ME intake exceeds that required to maintain weight (Fig 8). These figures also show that a substantial amount of feed or ME is required by the animal to maintain its present live weight unchanged. This is the maintenance requirement, and only ME in excess of this is available for productive purposes.

Protein

Protein is an essential component of all animal tissues. Even fatty tissue contains a small amount of protein in addition to chemical fat. In cattle nutrition, the protein concentration of the diet is more important than

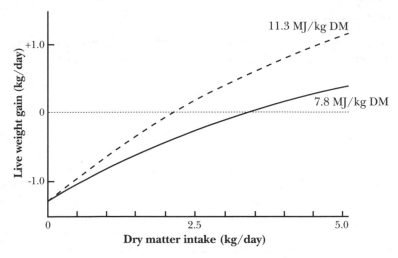

Fig 7   *Live weight change in 200 kg steers in relation to dry matter intake when eating diets of different metabolisable energy concentration*

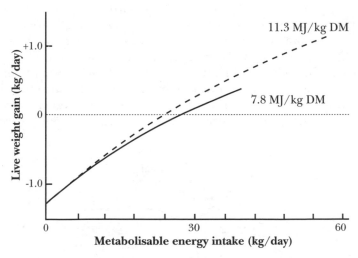

Fig 8   *Live weight change in 200 kg steers in relation to metabolisable energy intake when eating diets of different metabolisable energy concentration*

the absolute amount, because protein requirements vary with energy intake. In cattle feeds, protein is separated into that which is degradable or undegradable in the rumen (see the section on digestion below). The animal needs both rumen-degradable and rumen-undegradable protein.

21

Minerals and vitamins

Minerals and vitamins play an essential role in the growth and health of cattle. Further information can be found in *Ruminant Nutrition* in this series.

Roughage and concentrates

Cattle feed can be classified according to its fibre content into roughages (hay, crop residues and grazing) and concentrates. Roughages have a high fibre content (> 150 g/kg DM) and their ME concentration is usually less than 10 MJ/kg DM. Concentrates contain relatively little fibre (< 150 g/kg DM). Cereal grains and oilseed meals (ME > 10 MJ/kg DM) are the most common concentrates fed to beef cattle in the tropics. Some feedstuffs regarded as concentrates (e.g. citrus meal) are rich in cellulose but contain virtually no lignin, so they have a high ME value (> 11 MJ/kg DM) despite having a high crude fibre content.

Digestion in cattle

The bulk of cattle feed in the tropics is derived from natural and improved pastures, browse and crop residues, which contain a high proportion of fibre (ligno-cellulose). The productivity of cattle is therefore related to their ability to consume and digest the ligno-cellulose component of the diet. Cattle and other ruminants have three stomach compartments in addition to the abomasum or true stomach (Fig 9). The first two chambers (rumen and reticulum) function as a fermentation vat in which micro-organisms (bacteria, protozoa and fungi) break down carbohydrates and protein.

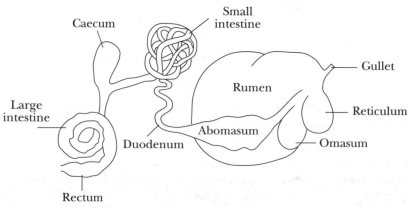

Fig 9   *The digestive system of a bovine*

Unlike non-ruminants, enzymes produced by rumen micro-organisms are able to break down ß-carbohydrates such as cellulose. The microbes also break down degradable protein to ammonia and amino acids. Fermentation in the rumen produces large quantities of volatile fatty acids (such as acetic, propionic and butyric acid). These are absorbed across the rumen wall and are the main source of energy for the animal. Microbial protein and protein that is not degraded in the rumen (rumen undegradable protein) are digested in the intestines and amino acids are absorbed across the intestinal wall.

Diet selection

Cattle are able to distinguish between feeds on the basis of taste, smell, texture and brightness. They learn to associate these characteristics with the consequences of eating the feeds concerned. Discomfort caused by toxins, nutrient deficiencies or excesses of specific nutrients (e.g. protein) cause the animals to select a different type of feed. Calves apparently learn to select appropriate forage when grazing with their mothers. By preferentially browsing on leafy material and avoiding plant stems, cattle grazing on tropical pastures tend to select a diet that has a higher protein content and is more digestible than the average of the herbage on offer. They also prefer feed that can be eaten quickly, even when the alternative is more nutritious.

Voluntary feed intake

The amount of feed an animal consumes is the greatest factor influencing its rate of growth. Accurate prediction of feed intake and an understanding of factors controlling it are therefore essential if beef production targets are to be achieved. Three different mechanisms set an upper limit to the feed intake of cattle in the tropics: rate of eating, rumen fill and metabolic control.

Rate of eating or bite size

Cattle will usually graze for a maximum of 12 hours, during which they take up to 38,000 bites. Herbage intake will be greater with a taller or denser sward than with a short, sparse one, since more herbage can be taken in with each bite (Table 8). Cattle are unable to graze grass shorter than about 10 mm. Bite size is also reduced when cattle feed selectively, for example when there is a low proportion of leaves to stems.

Table 8   Bite size, bites per day and organic matter intake of cows grazing
Setaria anceps **in relation to herbage and leaf density**

	Pasture 1	Pasture 2
Herbage density (kg/ha)	7440.0	3497.0
Leaf density (kg/ha)	2380.0	298.0
Bite size (mg OM/bite)	268.0	54.0
Total bites (per day)	29900.0	33700.0
OM intake (kg/day)	8.7	1.9

OM = organic matter
Source: Stobbs (1973a)

Rumen fill

Factors limiting the rate of digestion also influence total feed intake. There is a maximum amount of dry matter that can be held in the rumen and this varies between different animals. Most of the dry matter in the rumen is fibre. Voluntary intake increases with increasing: a) rumen volume; b) proportion of non-fibre components in the diet; c) fraction of degradable fibre; d) rate of fibre degradation; and e) outflow of particles to the abomasum. Rumen volume increases as a young animal grows but decreases as it approaches maturity due to accumulation of internal fat (Fig 10). This explains why voluntary feed intake reaches a maximum when animals are about 80 per cent of their mature weight. Advanced pregnancy also reduces effective rumen volume.

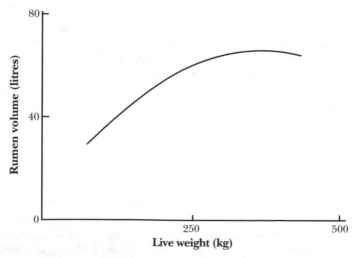

Fig 10   *Rumen volume in relation to live weight for a steer weighing 500 kg at maturity*

Young herbage is more easily digestible and has a higher protein content than older grasses. In addition, rumen microbial growth and the rate of digestion decline with a decrease in the protein content of the diet below 60 g/kg DM. Consequently, cattle eat less mature than young grass (Fig 11).

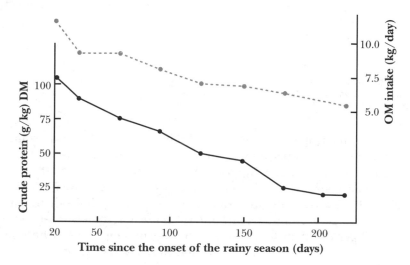

Fig 11   *Changes over time in crude protein content of standing herbage and organic matter intake by Mashona cows with an average weight of 350 kg (Elliott et al., 1961)*

Cattle will gain weight through eating mature grass (or hay of a low protein content and enhanced ME) when they are also given 0.25 or 0.5 kg/day of concentrates containing 30 to 50 per cent crude protein (Table 9). However, giving concentrates of 10 per cent or less protein (e.g. cereal grains) tends to depress the intake of roughage, although the supply of ME increases. Providing up to 2 kg/day of concentrates with 200 g crude protein/kg DM increases the intake of low protein roughage and the supply of ME by 2.5 times compared with animals subsisting on hay only. This phenomenon forms the basis of fattening using mature herbage or crop residues (see Chapter 8).

Metabolic control

Metabolic mechanisms limiting feed intake include thermoregulation, growth potential and lactation. Thermoregulation can have a consider-

Table 9   Predicted daily weight changes (kg/day) of 200 kg cattle

Crude protein content of concentrate (g/kg DM)	Amount of concentrate offered (kg/day)					
	0.00	0.25	0.50	1.00	1.50	2.00
	– 0.32					
100		– 0.19	– 0.07	0.12	0.26	0.36
200		– 0.08	0.12	0.41	0.58	0.65
300		0.01	0.23	0.43	*	*
400		0.08	0.28	*	*	*
500		0.13	0.26	*	*	*

*Feeding large amounts of concentrate with high protein contents is wasteful
Source: derived from the equations of Elliott (1967)

able effect in a tropical climate, since high ambient temperatures limit the amount of heat an animal can lose to the environment and may restrict feed intake. High temperatures have a greater effect on the feed intake of European type cattle than on the feed intake of native *Bos indicus* (Table 10). This table also illustrates the fact that some individuals have the potential to grow faster than others; they eat and metabolise more nutrients per day than their slower-growing contemporaries (the Friesians ate more and grew faster than the Brahmans, even at high temperatures).

Table 10   Effect of ambient temperature on the voluntary feed intake of heifers of different breeds (g DM/kg body weight/day)

Breed	17°C	38°C
Friesian (*B. taurus*)	29	25
Brahman (*B. indicus*)	24	22

Source: Colditz and Kellaway (1972)

Lactating cows eat more than dry cows of the same size. This is partly a result of an increase in rumen volume during lactation. When *Bos indicus* cows graze tropical rangeland, suckling cows consume 28 per cent more herbage than non-lactating animals of the same weight. However, they are not able to fully compensate for the demands of lactation, because the ME requirement of a cow producing 5 kg milk per day is approximately 50 per cent greater than that of a dry cow.

Protein/nitrogen

Pasture and crop residues used for feeding beef cattle in the tropics often lack essential nutrients. As pointed out above, diets with a low protein or non-protein nitrogen content lead to slow growth and low reproductive rates. Table 9 shows that young growing cattle grazing mature herbage during the dry season tended to lose less or gain more weight when offered a higher concentration of protein. Calving rates and calf weight at weaning are enhanced when a protein supplement (groundnut meal) is provided to breeding cows during the dry season (Table 11). The extra nitrogen could be provided as non-protein nitrogen (e.g. urea).

Table 11   Effects of supplementation with groundnut meal and a salt/mineral mix containing phosphorus on average productivity over six years of Mashona cows grazing *Hyparrhenia* spp. rangeland in Zimbabwe

| | Calving rate (%) | |
	No groundnut meal	Groundnut meal 0.9 kg/day
No salt/mineral mix	56.7	72.2
Salt/mineral mix[1]	61.7	76.7
	Calf body weight at weaning (kg)	
	No groundnut meal	Groundnut meal 0.9 kg/day
No salt/mineral mix	125.0	135.3
Salt/mineral mix[1]	138.1	146.2

1 Mixture of two parts mineral to one part salt, available *ad libitum* throughout
   the year; the final mix contained 6% phosphorus
Source: Ward (1968)

A deficiency of absorbed protein will occur even if the diet contains adequate digestible protein, if most of it is rumen-degradable and there is insufficient energy available to the microbes to enable them to synthesise microbial protein from the ammonia released by degradation of the dietary protein. For example, if pregnant cows consume insufficient ME to maintain weight and most of the protein in the diet is degradable, then the supply of protein to the developing foetus will be inadequate. This will lead to the birth of small calves. Newborn calf weight may be increased by providing small quantities (150 g/day) of a protein supplement that is relatively undegradable, such as blood meal or formaldehyde-treated oilseed meal, for the last six weeks of pregnancy.

Phosphorus

In many parts of the tropics, natural herbage is low in phosphorus, especially during the dry season. However, because phosphorus plays a role in energy metabolism, the greatest response to phosphorus supplements may occur among cattle grazing green grass during the rains, when intakes are highest. The most common symptom of phosphorus deficiency is a depraved appetite, when cattle will eat unusual items including old bones. If the bones are contaminated, the cattle may develop botulism. A lack of phosphorus is also expressed as slow growth and poor calving rates. Providing a phosphorus supplement (e.g. monocalcium phosphate) can improve growth and calving rates (Table 11).

Calcium

Calcium is essential for milk production and the growth of bones. Cattle in the tropics rarely suffer from calcium deficiency because most sources of roughage (e.g. grass, forage legumes and crop residues) contain adequate calcium. Cereal grains have a relatively low concentration of calcium, so diets comprising more than 60 per cent cereal-based concentrates require a limestone flour supplement.

Vitamin A

Green forage usually contains adequate ß-carotene, which is metabolised to vitamin A and stored in the liver. These reserves are normally sufficient to meet the animal's needs during the dry season. However, animals with a high energy intake require more vitamin A, and high concentrate diets should contain 3 million international units (i.u.) of vitamin A per tonne.

4 Growth and development

The growth and development of cattle are the main factors influencing the amount and quality of beef produced by a herd. Output can be quantified if the rate of off-take is known, together with the body weight and composition at slaughter (which determine the amount of edible meat produced). The rate of growth (increase in body weight with time) influences all these components. In Chapter 1 we have seen that off-take increases with an increase in calving rate and a reduction in the age at slaughter. An increase in growth rate leads to a reduction in age at slaughter, if carcasses of a specific weight range are required, or to an increase in carcass weight when animals are killed at a standard age. Furthermore, the value of a slaughter animal depends both on its size and on the relative proportions of muscle, fat and bone. The ideal carcass contains the maximum amount of muscle, a minimum of bone and an optimum proportion of fat, which may vary according to individual markets.

Mechanisms of growth

Knowledge of the mechanisms of growth allows the stockowner to slaughter his/her animals when they reach optimum size or body composition for a specific nutritional and/or economic environment. It also allows feeding and management to be planned to achieve the required body weight when prices are highest. Furthermore, the stockowner can evaluate the biological and economic implications of efforts to remedy under-nutrition and to manipulate body composition.

When an animal is given a highly digestible diet *ad libitum* from weaning to slaughter, a plot of body weight gain against time produces a sygmoid or S-shaped growth curve, where the rate of gain per day increases to a maximum at the point of inflection of the growth curve and then declines (Fig 12). In this example, the maximum rate of growth occurred when the

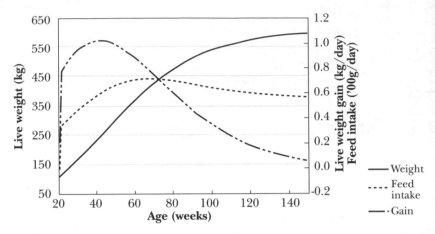

Fig 12   *Live weight and rate of gain of a steer from weaning to maturity when fed* ad libitum *on a diet of 68 per cent digestibility*

animal was 42 weeks old, when it weighed about 250 kg. When growth is expressed as energy retention, the reason for this pattern becomes clear. Feed or energy intake increases rapidly in very young animals, reaches a maximum, and then declines as the animal approaches its mature size. At the same time, there is an increase in the loss of energy given off as heat, mainly as a result of the increase in maintenance expenditure. The amount of energy retained in the body therefore declines. When metabolisable energy intake and heat loss are equal, the animal stops growing (Fig 13).

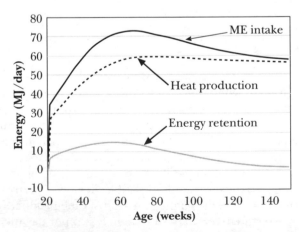

Fig 13   *Partition of metabolisable energy by a growing steer between heat production and storage as new tissue (gain)*

As the animal grows, the proportions of muscle, fat and bone change because of different patterns of growth of the different tissue types (Fig 14). The amount of muscle increases rapidly as the young animal grows, but the rate of increase becomes less as the animal approaches its mature weight. In contrast, the rate of increase of fat continues as the animal gains weight. The amount of muscle relative to bone also increases with live weight. Consequently, small young animals contain a very high proportion of bone, while very heavy animals will contain too much fat for some markets.

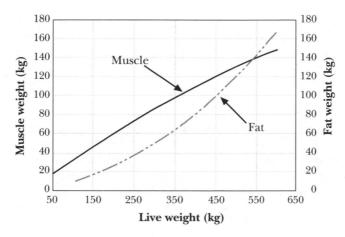

Fig 14 *Weights of muscle and fat in relation to live weight in a growing steer*

Improving efficiency of beef production

Rapid growth in cattle is associated with efficient conversion of the animal's feed to body weight. Table 12 illustrates the efficiency with which the growing animal converts the metabolisable energy of its feed to the energy of edible beef. However, the intake of metabolisable energy required to sustain a gain of 1.5 kg per day can only be achieved by feeding a diet containing a high proportion of grain. Even the most efficient system requires 7.8 kg grain and 1.1 kg protein concentrate for the production of 1 kg carcass weight gain. Increasing the rate of growth therefore increases energetic efficiency and can be achieved by other means such as light stocking rates.

It is also possible to estimate the efficiency of conversion of fossil fuel energy to beef energy. Intensive systems will use large amounts of fossil

31

Table 12   Efficiency of conversion of feed energy by beef steers gaining body weight at different rates

Rate of weight gain (kg/day)	Metabolisable energy intake (MJ/day)	Yield of energy metabolisable by humans (MJ/day)	Feed energy recovered for human consumption (%)
1.5	110.0	18.6	16.9
0.2	51.0	3.1	6.1

Source: Smith (1981)

fuel to power tractors and for the manufacture of fertilizers, pesticides and livestock feed. It has been estimated that the efficiency (E) of use of such support energy for intensive animal production (milk, lamb, broilers and eggs) in the United Kingdom was 0.11–0.62 where

$$E = \frac{\text{Gross energy in product}}{\text{Support energy input}}$$

Beef production by subsistence farmers in the tropics may use very little support energy (in the form of grain or cultivated forage), so the efficiency of use of fossil fuel is much higher than in intensive systems and may be as high as 10–50, in spite of the low level of output. Furthermore, in extensive systems of beef production, cattle subsist on crop residues and on natural grazing land that is unsuitable for cultivation. One of the criticisms of extensive beef production is its perceived low efficiency, but actually it uses limited external inputs very efficiently. Stockowners in the tropics can often increase the efficiency of beef production by making small changes, such as introducing supplementary feeding or reducing the age at which the animals are slaughtered. Off-take is a useful index of the efficiency of beef production. It is influenced by the production system, the herd structure and the production characteristics (e.g. calving, mortality and growth rates).

Intensive beef production is only feasible in countries that produce a large grain surplus, have large quantities of by-products of agro-industries (e.g. sugar cane or cotton) and have adequate rainfall or irrigation and the resources to purchase or manufacture fertilizers and establish planted pastures. In most countries in Africa, the price of beef is normally less than four times the price of grain and therefore the feeding of grain to cattle is seldom profitable (see Table 13).

The production of beef from extensive rangeland and poor quality crop residues may be enhanced by:

Table 13   Profit margins in beef fattening as a percentage of gross output

Price ratios maize/beef	Feeder steer price as % of fat steer price				
	60	70	80	90	100
1:10	23	17	8	0	– 7
1:9	21	15	6	– 2	– 9
1:8	18	12	3	– 4	– 12
1:7	15	9	0	– 7	– 17
1:6	11	5	– 14	– 11	– 19
1:5	5	1	– 10	– 17	– 25
1:4	– 4	– 10	– 19	– 26	– 34

Source: Schaefer-Kehnert (1981)

- supplementary feeding to correct protein and mineral deficiencies;
- keeping suitable cattle genotypes;
- controlling diseases and parasites; and
- reducing calf mortality and increasing calving rate and pre-weaning growth.

The output and quality of beef from small-scale multi-purpose herds could be increased by: a) improving the calving rate and reducing the mortality rate; b) finishing/fattening cows and draught animals at the end of their productive or working lives (e.g. using crop residues as a basis for stall-feeding); and c) selling surplus animals when they have reached the desired weight.

The efficiency of beef production depends on the amounts of muscle and fat produced in relation to the total amount of feed eaten. Muscle weight increases rapidly as cumulative feed intake increases in young animals. However, as the animal approaches maturity, further increases in feed consumption result in progressively smaller increases in muscle weight (Fig 15).

When animals graze natural or improved pastures, the amount they eat increases with the time spent grazing. Stockowners should therefore aim to optimise grazing time by allowing grazing early in the morning and late in the afternoon. Cattle should also be fed at a high level when they are young (up to approx. 9 months). Cattle should be slaughtered as soon as they achieve their optimum muscle mass (approx. 120 kg muscle, or 450 kg live weight), since keeping them longer results in a substantial increase in the amount of fat in the carcass with little extra muscle. They will also consume feed that would be better used by small young animals. The smaller animals should be retained if forage or adequate grazing is available, since they will respond by producing additional muscle.

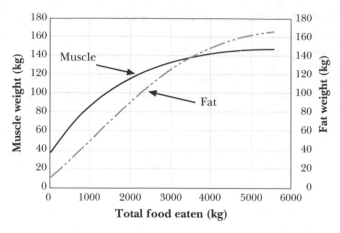

Fig 15   *Growth of fat and protein in relation to cumulative feed intake*

Effect of mature size on growth rate and body composition

When animals that have the potential to achieve different mature live weights are offered the same highly digestible feed *ad libitum* from weaning to maturity, the one that is largest at maturity and eats the most grows fastest (Fig 16). When the two animals are compared at the same live weight, the one that will be heaviest at maturity will contain the least fat. The implications of these findings for beef cattle breeding are discussed in Chapter 5.

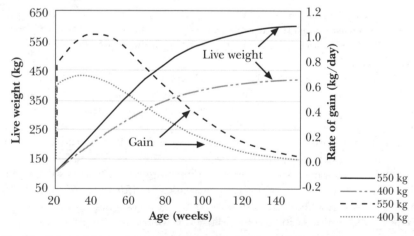

Fig 16   *Live weights and rates of gain of cattle of different mature weights*

Effect of sex on growth rate and carcass composition

In herds where calving rates are high (> 70 per cent), heifers surplus to breeding requirements will be available for slaughter and cows will be slaughtered at the end of their optimum reproductive lives. When given the same diet, steers grow faster than heifers (Table 14). Among animals of the same breed, heifers contain more fat than steers of the same body weight. Even though heifers are smaller than steers when mature, they still contain a higher proportion of fat. This means that heifers should be lighter than steers at slaughter if their carcasses are to contain the optimum proportion of fat.

Table 14 Weights of Afrikaner steers and heifers grazing semi-arid rangeland

Age	Steers' weight (kg)	Heifers' weight (kg)
Weaning	173.9	159.6
18 months	266.9	240.5
27 months	311.0	282.8

Source: Richardson and Khaka (1981)

Intact bulls grow faster than castrates and, if fattened on high-energy diets and slaughtered when young, they produce high quality carcasses. At a carcass weight of 205 kg, bull carcasses contain only 18 per cent fat compared to 24 per cent in steers. Growth rates on rangeland are slower, and bulls develop undesirable secondary sex characteristics such as a heavy crest and coarse-textured dark flesh before they attain the optimum pre-slaughter weight. They may also become sexually active. It is therefore advisable to castrate all male animals not required for breeding if they are to be kept on rangeland.

Effect of pregnancy and lactation on growth and carcass composition

Pregnant heifers grazing on rangeland gain more maternal weight than their unmated contemporaries. Table 15 shows that, if slaughtered at 155 days after conception, they produce heavier carcasses than those that are either unmated or 274 days pregnant. This is probably due to hormone activity. The thickness of fat over the *Longissimus dorsi* muscle and the cross-sectional area of the muscle are indicators of the amounts of fat and muscle in the carcass respectively. The effects of pregnancy on

Table 15 Live weight gains, pre-slaughter weights, carcass weights and fat thickness of heifers[1]

	Not mated	155 days pregnant	274 days pregnant	83 days after calving	192 days after calving
Live weight gain (kg)	145.6	163.0	175.1	95.8	56.9
Pre-slaughter weight (kg)	449.1	470.9	478.9	396.8	350.4
Cold carcass weight (kg)	225.2	233.7	225.7	186.7	155.5
Fat thickness (mm)	9.8	10.2	11.3	5.7	0.2
Rib eye muscle cross section area (mm)	635.8	625.1	610.7	526.4	502.4

1 All heifers grazed as one herd for 474 days; were given the same supplementary feed; and were slaughtered on the same day
Source: Richardson and Thomson (1984)

fat thickness and area of the rib eye muscle are small but lactation has a substantial negative effect. The effects of pregnancy can be used to advantage when heifers are managed intensively. Heifers that are being fattened for slaughter may be mated prior to penning them in a feedlot, since they grow faster than non-pregnant animals and their feeding behaviour is not affected by oestrus.

Lactation causes a large reduction in pre-slaughter live weight and cold carcass weight and the extent of this effect increases with the length of lactation. The carcasses of lactating heifers contain the least fat and muscle of any cattle. Heifers grazing tropical rangeland cannot obtain sufficient nutrients to sustain both growth and lactation and are likely to produce a carcass with too little muscle and fat.

Effects of under-nutrition on growth

Degrees of under-nutrition range from a mild reduction in intake below that of animals given a high-energy diet *ad libitum* to long periods of severe under-nutrition due to insufficient forage. Where rainfall is seasonal and variable, grazing cattle are likely to face intermittent periods of moderate or severe under-nutrition due to the shortage or low protein content of available forage.

Undernourished immature cattle grow slowly during periods of nutritional deprivation and will take longer to reach their optimum slaughter condition. In severe conditions, they survive by mobilising fat and protein accrued when feed was plentiful and will consequently lose weight

(Fig 17). These cattle will take a long time to reach slaughter weight. When cattle are gaining weight, the body weight, rate of growth and feed intake are interrelated and determine the efficiency of growth. Compensatory growth is abnormally rapid growth relative for age that is observed when under-nutrition ceases and animals are liberally fed.

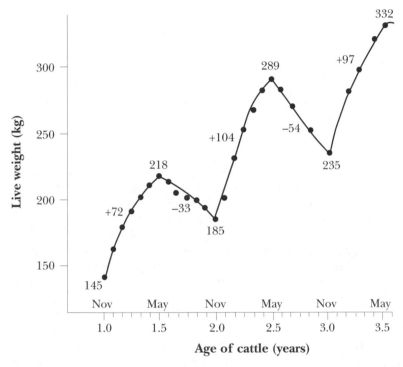

Fig 17   *Seasonal live weight changes in cattle grazing native pasture at Katherine, Northern Australia (Osborn, 1976). Similar growth patterns are seen in cattle kept under semi-arid conditions in Zambia and Zimbabwe*

In one trial, Hereford steers 9–10 months old weighing 250 kg were given a complete diet with 50 per cent roughage either *ad libitum* for 419 days or in restricted amounts for 89 days and then *ad libitum* for a recovery period of 330 days. Steers lost 16.4 per cent of their initial weight during the period of restriction and were 141 kg lighter than the controls at the end of the restriction period. During recovery, the restricted steers showed compensatory growth and almost caught up with their unrestricted counterparts (Table 16). The practical implication is that if high quality feed or grazing will be plentiful following a period of under-nutrition, animals may be allowed to lose weight during a period of feed

Table 16   Live weights, empty body weights and the proportions of protein and fat in the carcass

| | Feed allocation during first 89 days of experiment | |
	Ad libitum	Restricted
Initial live weight (kg)	251	250
Live weight after 89 days (kg)	350	209
Final live weight (kg)	602	584
Empty body weight (kg)	504	483
Protein in empty body (g/kg)	153	156
Fat in empty body (g/kg)	350	342

Source: Ryan et al. (1993)

scarcity, especially if supplementary feed is expensive. However, compensatory growth will not occur unless animals are able to eat large quantities of a highly digestible diet.

Postnatal under-nutrition does not affect the capacity of cattle to reach normal mature size. Seasonal under-nutrition may be reduced by providing the cattle with supplementary feed in the form of concentrates or conserved forages. In the long term, light stocking rates (number of LSU/ha) reduce the incidence of under-nutrition except during years of abnormally low rainfall.

However, when very young animals are undernourished, the resulting differences in live weight persist for a very long time, even when all animals subsequently have access to a higher plane of nutrition. The male calves of cows that were stocked at 0.37 cows/ha were 39.6 kg lighter when weaned at nine months than those whose dams were stocked at 0.123 cows/ha. The difference was caused by the lower milk yields of cows kept at a high stocking density. This difference persisted almost unchanged until the steers were slaughtered at 31 months old, irrespective of post-weaning treatment (Table 17). Therefore, when there is limited availability of feed resources, cows suckling young calves should be given priority.

The adverse effects of under-nutrition in early life persist for longer than those of severe deprivation at a later stage due to the relationship between live weight, feed intake and rate of gain (see Fig 12 on page 30). In the very young animal (maximum rate of feed intake has yet to be reached), intake increases with live weight. If under-nutrition occurs during this stage, once feed becomes plentiful again, these animals will eat less than their larger, well-fed contemporaries and will either grow at the same rate or slower than them. If feed restriction is imposed later in

Table 17 Final live weights (kg) of 31-month-old steers subjected to different stocking rates before and after weaning and with or without supplementary feeding during the last 90 days before slaughter

Post-weaning stocking rate (head/ha)	Stocking rate of dams 0.37 cows/ha	Stocking rate of dams 0.123 cows/ha	Range + 21% CP cubes	Range only	Mean live weight (kg)
0.37	350.0	394.9	385.9	359.9	373.5
0.22	368.9	398.6	398.9	371.6	385.2
Range + cubes	372.5	409.9			392.1
Range only	343.9	383.6			365.8
Mean live weight (kg)	358.9	396.8			

CP = crude protein
Source: Richardson and Khaka (1983)

life (animals aged 12 months or older), then when feed becomes plentiful after the period of under-nutrition, previously well-nourished and under-nourished animals will eat similar amounts (and the latter may eat more). The lightest animals will have the lowest maintenance requirement and energy cost per unit of gain, and consequently they will grow the fastest and exhibit compensatory growth. It is therefore advisable to avoid, if at all possible, the under-nutrition of beef cattle when they are young because the adverse effects persist for up to three years (they probably disappear as the animal approaches its final mature weight). Under-nutrition in later life, for example during the dry season, is less of a problem because cattle can exhibit compensatory growth when the grass grows during the rainy season.

5 Breeds and breeding

Selective breeding of domestic cattle has led to the development of many different breeds throughout the world. The objective of breeding beef cattle is to produce animals that can optimise their reproduction, growth and carcass quality within the local environment. As a general rule, traditional cattle that have evolved in a particular environment are the ones that do best in that environment. If a farming system is changed, it may be desirable to change the genotype of the cattle and this is most rapidly achieved by crossbreeding. However, there may be unwelcome side effects. The cattle may prove to be less disease resistant or their teeth may be unable to cope with tough pasture grasses. Breeding animals that will grow faster and produce 'better' carcasses may be desirable in dedicated beef enterprises but may well be totally counter-productive for many of the cattle production systems found in Africa, the Pacific and the Caribbean. For example, animals that have the potential to grow faster are usually larger than native ones and therefore less able to survive periods of drought. In addition, most stockowners in the tropics are not breeding for beef production alone but for multiple uses including milk and draught power. Further information can be found in *Animal Breeding* in this series.

Breeds of beef cattle

Cattle belonging to one breed have a similar appearance and have usually been deliberately selected to perform well in a certain region of the world. In the tropics, breeds have been developed for different climates, available nutrition, disease challenges and production systems. Indigenous breeds have evolved over a long period of time and are best suited to traditional production systems in their local regions. If conditions change (e.g. by introducing supplementary feeding and/or improved health care), a different breed might perform better in that location.

Cattle are divided into two species: *Bos taurus* (humpless, European cattle) and *Bos indicus* (humped, indigenous cattle) but these can interbreed to produce fertile offspring. *Bos indicus* breeds are classified into two main groups: Sanga and Zebu.

Sanga cattle

These have a relatively small cervico-thoracic hump, are indigenous to eastern and southern Africa and include the Afrikaner (Fig 18), Ankole, Barotse, Dinka, Mashona, Nguni, Nkone, Ovambo, Tswana and Tuli. Average mature cows weigh between 350 kg for the Mashona to 550 kg for the Tuli. On rangeland, calving rates are generally over 70 per cent, although 60 per cent is more common for Afrikaner cows (see Maule, 1990 and Payne and Hodges, 1997 for more information).

Fig 18   *Afrikaner cow, South Africa*

Zebu breeds

Zebu breeds are characterised by large thoracic humps. They include the Angoni, Boran, Brahman (Fig 19), Gudali, Gyr, Karamajong, Kehdah-Kelantan, Madagascar Zebu, Nellore, Small East African Zebu, Tuareg and White Fulani.

Small West African breeds

Bos taurus cattle are normally associated with the British Isles and Western Europe, however, taurine cattle of ancient origin are found in West Africa (e.g. the N'Dama, Fig 20). The N'Dama may be the oldest domesticated

Fig 19   *Brahman bull in Malaysia*

breed in Africa and it is acclimatised to life on the edge of the tropical rain forest. Individuals are normally trypanotolerant, but they may succumb to trypanosomiasis when under stress (e.g. when lactating, working or suffering from under-nutrition). Other taurine breeds found in West Africa include the Bakosi, Baoule, Forest Muturu and West African Shorthorn (Fig 21).

Fig 20   *N'Dama cattle in Ghana*

42

Fig 21   *West African Shorthorn in Nigeria*

British beef breeds

British beef breeds fatten readily on good quality grazing or in the feedlot
and have been used for crossbreeding in the tropics. Aberdeen Angus is
a popular breed since the cows are probably the most fertile of this group,
but it is generally the slowest growing of any British breed. The Sussex is
another popular beef breed, as is the Hereford (Fig 22), but Herefords
are not well adapted to grazing tropical grasses. In a 16-year experiment
on semi-arid rangeland in Zimbabwe, only 45 per cent of Hereford calves
survived to three years of age (compared with 82 per cent of indigenous

Fig 22   *Hereford bull*

43

calves). A high proportion of the Hereford deaths were associated with inability to feed properly due to excessive wear and loss of the temporary incisors before the permanent teeth erupted.

Large European breeds

Carcasses of large European breeds, e.g. Charolais, Limousin (Fig 23), Main Anjou and Simmental, contain more muscle and less fat than carcasses of British breeds of similar weights. This is possibly because, until recently, they were selected to be dual-purpose draught and beef animals. The British beef breeds were selected solely for beef characteristics because horses were the principal draught animals. Calving difficulties are fairly common in the large European breeds. At Matopos in Zimbabwe, Charolais heifers frequently had calving problems but the local Nkone heifers had none, irrespective of the size of the sire (which included Charolais).

Fig 23   *Limousin cow*

Caribbean and Pacific

There are no indigenous breeds of cattle in the West Indies or the Pacific islands. Locally adapted crossbreeds include the Jamaica Black and Jamaica Brahman. The Senepol breed was developed in the Virgin Islands specifically to meet the needs of the tropical beef producer.

Genotype–environment interaction

Beef breeds selected for their superior performance in one environment will not necessarily be superior in a different environment. This is known as genotype–environment interaction. One breed can only be accurately compared with another if they are both subjected to the same conditions of environment, feeding and management. An experiment in south-west Zimbabwe compared cows of different breeds grazing together and found that Mashona cows had the highest calving rate and the lightest calves at weaning, while Brahman cows weaned the heaviest calves and produced the greatest weight of weaned calf per cow per year (Table 18). As maintenance expenditure and feed intake of breeding cows are related to their live weight, cow productivity should be expressed as output per 100 kg of cow. On this basis, Mashona cows (indigenous to Zimbabwe) were the most efficient, while Afrikaner, Charolais and Sussex were the least efficient.

Table 18 Average performance of purebred cows in Zimbabwe over three years

Breed type (sub-species) Breed	Sanga Afrikaner	Sanga Mashona	Zebu Brahman	*B. taurus* Charolais	*B. taurus* Sussex
Average number of cow records per year	87	53	21	28	39
Calving rate (%)	55.5±3.0	76.0±3.8	70.0±3.8	67.0±5.0	60.0±4.3
Calf survival (%)	83.3±3.0	89.1±3.2	82.5±4.6	81.9±4.1	83.7±3.9
Calf weight at weaning (kg)	183.9±2.1	171.9±2.2	206.8±3.1	186.4±2.9	177.6±2.7
Weaned calf (kg/cow/year)	89.1	121.2	130.3	107.2	93.4
Cow weight at weaning (kg)	355.3	325.4	389.6	452.6	386.5
Weaned calf (kg/100 kg of cow/year)	24.0	36.9	32.4	24.0	23.5

Note: Cows were not culled for any reason, but those that died were not replaced. Consequently, the averages were not whole numbers, but have been rounded up or down to the nearest whole number
Source: Tawonezvi et al. (1988a)

Table 19 illustrates the genotype–environment interaction, showing that 75 per cent Limousin/25 per cent Aberdeen Angus steers gained more weight than purebred Angus when stocked at 2.25 steers/ha on a fertilized pasture, but at a stocking rate of 4.13 steers/ha, Angus steers gained the most weight. Apparently, at a high stocking rate, the large crossbreds were unable to obtain sufficient nutrients to meet their requirements for maintenance and sustain a rapid growth rate.

Table 19   Mean body weight gains by steers of two genotypes grazing *Festuca arundinacea* pastures at different stocking rates

Steer genotype	Stocking rate 2.25 steers/ha kg/steer/day	kg/ha	Stocking rate 4.13 steers/ha kg/steer/day	kg/ha
Aberdeen Angus	0.51 ± 0.08	1.16	0.43 ± 0.04	1.77
75% Limousin 25% Angus	0.65 ± 0.08	1.47	0.33 ± 0.07	1.34

Source: Mezzadra et al. (1992)

Multiple interactions between factors affecting productivity mean it is difficult to determine by experiment the optimum breeds and types for different biological and economic environments. The problem is compounded in developing countries, where cows are often expected to rear a calf, produce milk for human consumption and even pull a plough, so imposing additional management variables. Furthermore, rainfall and herbage production vary widely between years and grass growth is affected by soil type. More work is needed to help scientists fully understand the mechanisms of genotype–environment interactions and thus why one breed is the most productive in one environment but not in another.

Fig 24 shows the factors that influence each other and the relationship between the animal and its environment. In particular, note how energy expenditure on maintenance, feed intake, milk production and growth rate are all interrelated. Stockowners should therefore take care to select an appropriate breed of cattle to suit beef production in their own particular circumstances. A good general rule is that local cattle survive best in their own environment. If the level of management improves, then it may be possible to crossbreed local animals with beef breeds imported from temperate regions.

Feed intake and maintenance

Differences in performance between breeds when given the same diet are a result of differences in voluntary feed intake, ability to digest the

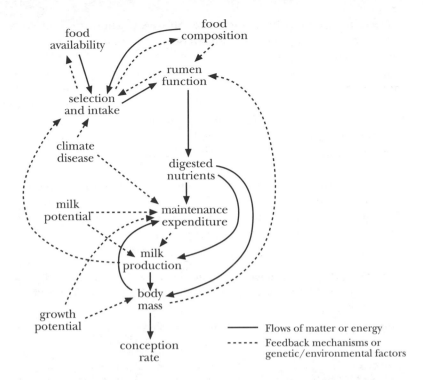

food
availability

food
composition

rumen
function

selection
and intake

climate
disease

digested
nutrients

milk
potential

maintenance
expenditure

milk
production

growth
potential

body
mass

conception
rate

——— Flows of matter or energy

- - - - - Feedback mechanisms or
genetic/environmental factors

Fig 24   *Relationships between the components of cattle productivity and the environment*

feed and maintenance expenditure. When Brahman and Hereford x
Shorthorn steers were given low quality pasture hay, both breeds effectively maintained the same live weight (246 kg). However, Hereford x
Shorthorn animals ate 20 per cent more hay than the Brahmans. This
may be due partly to the lower energy requirement for maintenance of
the Brahman cattle (indicated by the their lower fasting metabolism)
and by their superior ability to digest low quality forage (both factors
that enhance survival during drought). When the diet was changed to
high quality lucerne (alfalfa) hay, the British crossbreds ate the most hay
and gained the most weight. The study shows that cattle with a high
potential growth rate or milk yield have a higher maintenance requirement than low potential animals, but they can achieve a higher rate of
gain when fed a high quality diet.

Differences between breeds and between animals within breeds in their
voluntary feed intake and capacity to digest low quality roughage are
rarely considered when selecting suitability of genotypes for developing
countries. Most comparative breed trials measuring feed intake and feed
conversion are based on a complete diet containing no more than 30 per
cent roughage *ad libitum*, or protein-rich concentrates in addition to

47

mature low-protein fibrous herbage. However, when the diet consists entirely of mature grass hay (around 5 per cent crude protein), Brahman steers are able to digest feed in the rumen more rapidly than Herefords. It appears that Brahman steers eating low-protein roughage transfer more urea from the blood to the rumen, leading to a higher concentration of ammonia in the rumen fluid. Consequently, Brahmans exhibit a better rate of digestion (K_d) and digestibility of low-protein diets than Herefords (Table 20). However, feeding cattle protein-rich supplements limits the transfer of nitrogen to the rumen, leading to negligible differences in rumen ammonia and rate of digestion. Zebu cattle tend to have a larger rumen volume in relation to weight than British breeds. This is associated with a slow rate of outflow of digesta from the rumen. Consequently, feed remains in the rumen for a longer time and the digestibility of low quality roughages is enhanced.

Table 20   Effect of breed type on rumen ammonia concentration, digestion rate and digestibility of mature *Digitaria decumbens* hay (4.94% crude protein)

Breed type	Rumen ammonia (mg/l)	Digestion rate (K_d)	Digestibility
Bos taurus (Hereford)	16 ±2.4	0.023 ±0.003	0.43
Bos indicus (Brahman)	40 ±2.9	0.045 ±0.003	0.50

Six animals of each breed
Source: Hunter and Siebert (1985)

Resistance to diseases and parasites

Indigenous breeds are generally more tolerant than exotic animals to tropical diseases and parasites (e.g. the trypanotolerant N'Dama). Ticks are common parasites in the tropics and limit cattle productivity through loss of blood, infected tick bites and irritation. They transmit diseases (e.g. anaplasmosis and theileriosis) and are associated with dematophilosis. Productivity decreases as the number of ticks on the animal increases. *Bos indicus* cattle carry lower tick burdens than European animals, but West African *Bos taurus* breeds (e.g. N'Dama) are even less affected since they are resistant to ticks. Trials in Australia showed that yearling Brahman bulls carried significantly fewer maturing ticks than Hereford x Shorthorn bulls of the same age. In western Ethiopia, indigenous Horro cattle carried substantially fewer ticks than Borans (Table 21), indicating a difference in tick resistance between the two *Bos indicus* breeds. The crossbred Horro x Friesians were very susceptible to ticks.

Table 21   Mean tick burdens of different cattle breeds and crosses

Genotype	*Boophilus decoloratus*	Total tick burden (no. ticks per animal)
Pure Horro	16.3[a]	21.5[a]
Horro × Friesian	162.5[c]	188.0[c]
Pure Boran	55.9[b]	69.2[b]
Boran × Friesian	58.6[b]	88.3[b]

a,b,c Values in the same column having different superscripts are significantly
    different ($P < 0.05$)
Source: Adapted from de Castro (1991)

Selection within breeds

Selection is the process of choosing some bulls and cows rather than
others as parents of the next generation. The objective is to improve the
performance of beef cattle, especially in terms of fertility, growth rate
and carcass quality. Good breeding and production records are needed
to identify the most productive animals and selection efforts will take
several years to achieve a substantial increase in productivity. Because
one bull produces more progeny than one cow, it is especially important
to select superior bulls (see *Animal Breeding* in this series). The effect of
selection on productivity is determined by selection differential, heritability and generation interval.

Selection differential

This refers to the fact that a greater difference in production between
selected parents and the herd mean will lead to a better response to
selection.

Heritability (h^2)

This is the degree of superiority of the parents (over the herd average)
that is passed on to their offspring. If the heritability of a trait is high,
there will be a greater response to selection than if it is low. Heritability
varies between traits and the heritability of a specific trait is also influenced by the environment. Traits with low heritabilities (5–12 per cent)
include calving rate and calf survival; traits with moderate heritability
(15–35 per cent) include birth weight, weaning weight, feed intake and
feed conversion; and traits with high heritability (35–60 per cent) include
eye muscle area and fat thickness (in carcasses of similar weight) and
mature weight.

Generation interval

The generation interval is the average age of the parents when the off-spring that will replace them in the breeding herd are born. In cattle, the generation interval may be long (e.g. over six years) in herds subjected to poor nutrition, because calving rates are low and age at first calving is high. An increase in generation interval reduces the rate at which productivity can be improved by selection.

Selecting individuals for specific traits

Growth rate

Growth rate or weight at a given age or stage of life (e.g. weaning) is easily recorded and is moderately heritable. Breeders therefore often select for growth rate as a means of increasing beef production. Selection of Aberdeen Angus cattle kept on pasture for either fast (high-line) or slow (low-line) growth from birth to 12 months of age for four generations resulted in a difference of 30 per cent between lines in live weight of progeny at 12 months (Table 22). Selection for an increase in growth rate at one stage leads to an increase in live weight at all ages, including that of mature breeding cows. In this case, the breeding stock were selected in the same environment in which their progeny were kept and the increase in growth rate in the high-line reflects the enhanced efficiency of the selected animals. This was a result of their lower

Table 22 Response to selection over four generations

	Selection line		
	High **(fast growth)**	**Control**	**Low** **(slow growth)**
Birth weight (kg)	30.7	29.0	24.6
Weaning weight (kg)	201.0	185.0	157.0
Yearling weight (kg)	268.0	250.0	203.0
Milk production (kg/day)	6.5	6.3	5.8
Cow live weight (kg)	489[a] ±11.0	457[b] ±9.0	394[c] ±13.0
ME for cow maintenance (MJ/cow/day)[1]	46.5 ±1.5	43.7 ±2.2	45.7 ±2.1
ME for cow maintenance (MJ/W$^{0.75}$/day)[2]	0.45[a] ±0.01	0.44[a] ±0.02	0.52[b] ±0.02

1 ME is metabolisable energy
2 W 0.75 represents metabolic body weight of the cow
a,b,c Means for selection lines with different superscripts are significantly
     different ($P < 0.05$)
Source: Herd (1995)

maintenance requirement per kg $W^{0.75}$. Since the increase in cow size did not cause a rise in maintenance ME per cow, the same stocking density could be kept.

A trial in Queensland, Australia showed that selection for high growth rate in cattle grazing tropical pasture (with minimal control of parasites) can lead to a decrease in fasting metabolism. However, animals in the control (random mated) and selected lines had similar growth rates when fed lucerne hay *ad libitum* in pens. Selection should therefore take place in the environment where the animals will be expected to perform.

Calving rate

In Chapter 2 (Table 5) we saw that calving rate has a major effect on the number of slaughter animals produced. Thus, an improvement in fertility in breeds that have a low average calving rate in the tropics (e.g. the Afrikaner) would be an effective means of improving beef production. Genetic improvement in fertility through selection is difficult because the heritability of calving rate is low (< 15 per cent) and several calvings per cow are needed to identify highly fertile individuals. However, variability is often high and progress may be achieved. For example, stringent culling of infertile females in a closed Afrikaner herd in Zimbabwe resulted in an increase in calving rate from 66 per cent to 78 per cent in two generations. This was partly an indirect response to selection for live weight prior to first mating, since the heavier cows had higher conception rates. A similar response to selection has been found in a Droughtmaster (part Brahman, part Shorthorn) herd in Australia, and the response was reflected in the progeny.

Disease resistance

Selection for tick resistance has been successful in the tropical regions of Australia, where the use of tick-resistant bulls is recommended. However, in those regions, there is only one species of economic importance (*Boophilus microplus*). In Africa, cattle face the challenge of several tick species, and animals resistant to some species may not be resistant to others.

Progeny testing

Progeny testing is evaluation of a sire according to the performance of his progeny and is the most accurate method of measuring the breeding value of a bull. However, only a small number of bulls can be tested because each must be mated to 20–30 cows. The cows and their progeny are kept in similar environments. Only progeny testing can measure the bull's ability to breed heifers that are more fertile than their contemporaries and have the ability to rear heavy weaned calves.

Group breeding schemes can overcome the problems of effective selection and progeny testing in small herds (Fig 25). Participating breeders provide females selected on the basis of their superior performance (and the performance of other relatives such as half-sisters) to an 'elite' nucleus herd, which may be established on a co-operative or government farm. Male progeny of the nucleus herd are evaluated on the basis of their own performance or by progeny testing. Bulls identified as superior are then made available to co-operating members. Management and nutrition in the nucleus herd should be similar to that in members' herds.

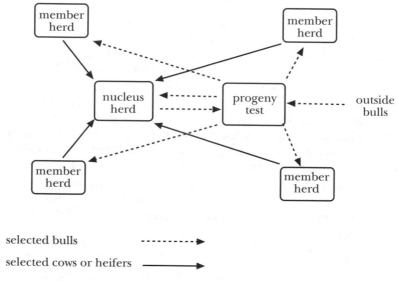

Fig 25   *Structure of a group breeding scheme*

Crossbreeding

Crossbreeding has been used in many parts of the world as a means of increasing the productivity of beef cattle, especially in commercial herds (Fig 26). While indigenous breeds are often well adapted to a specific region and production system, changing the genotype can bring about an increase in performance, especially if nutrition is improved and/or diseases controlled by vaccination. Compared with selection, crossbreeding can bring about rapid genetic change and it is far more cost-effective than replacing the herd with animals of a new breed. Crossbreeding can change the genotype of cattle in a herd within a timescale of 3–5 years and will often improve the efficiency of production. However,

Fig 26   *Sussex × Mashona cattle in a commercial herd in Zimbabwe*

genotypes should be matched to production strategies and to environmental and economic conditions.

Productivity per cow may increase by up to 15 per cent in Zebu × British cows compared with purebred Zebus. One of the objectives of crossbreeding is to maximise the inherent strengths of the parent breeds and to minimise their weaknesses. For example, the fertility of an indigenous breed may be combined with the rapid growth rate of a British breed. In addition, heterosis or hybrid vigour may provide an additional bonus. Heterosis is the difference between the performance of the crossbred progeny and the average of the two parent breeds when kept in the same environment. In a trial in Botswana, the progeny of Tswana cows sired by Simmental and Brahman bulls were heavier at 18 months than those sired by Afrikaner and Tswana bulls (Table 23). This was true for animals kept on fenced government-run ranches or under traditional management on

Table 23   Mean weights of purebred Tswana cattle (kg) and crossbred animals from Tswana dams at 18 months under improved (ranch) and traditional (cattle post) management

Breed of sire	Cattle post	Ranch
Tswana	233[a] (26)	273[a] (26)
Afrikaner	228[a] (29)	279[a] (22)
Simmental	265[b] (29)	335[b] (25)
Brahman	259[b] (34)	326[b] (24)

a,b Means in the same column with different superscripts are significantly
     different ($P < 0.05$); numbers of animals of each breed shown in brackets
     Source: Trail et al. (1977)

communal grazing. These results show that herd productivity may be enhanced by using sires of a breed with a high potential for growth (such as Simmental) for the production of steers and heifers for slaughter. The effects of such crossing are approximately double under good ranch conditions compared with cattle post conditions (communal grazing with individually owned cattle kept in owners' corrals overnight).

The wider the genetic difference between the parent breeds, the greater the likelihood that hybrid vigour will be manifested; i.e. crossing a Sanga with a British breed will increase production to a greater extent than crossing two British breeds. Comparison of reciprocal crosses between Sussex and Afrikaner with their purebred parent breeds shows that the crossbred cows are far more productive than purebreds (Table 24). Heterosis for calving rate is 16.9 per cent and that for cow productivity is 24.9 per cent. However, hybrid vigour may not be the only explanation. When European and tropical breeds are crossed, the superiority of the crossbred animals over both parents is often due to the fact that purebred European cattle simply cannot survive in the tropical environment. This apparent heterosis effect may therefore derive from a genotype–environment interaction rather than from inheritance. The values of heterosis for reciprocal crosses between Sanga breeds and between Sanga and Zebu breeds were far smaller than those between Sussex and Afrikaner. Although the productivity index of both the reciprocal crosses was higher than that of both parent breeds, none of the crossbred genotypes in this study were more productive than the best purebred, the Mashona (see Table 18). Stockowners should therefore make adequate assessment of

Table 24 **Components of productivity of purebred and crossbred cows, with estimates of heterosis**

Cow genotype	Calving rate (%)	Calf weight at weaning (kg)	Cow productivity (weight of weaned calf/ 100 kg of cow/year)
Afrikaner (87)	55.5 ±3.0	183.9 ±2.1	24.0 ±0.5
Sussex (39)	60.0 ±4.3	177.6 ±2.7	23.5 ±2.3
Africaner bull x Sussex cow (35)	66.7 ±4.5	197.5 ±2.7	29.1 ±2.3
Sussex bull x Africaner cow (56)	66.4 ±3.6	198.4 ±2.2	29.8 ±1.8
Heterosis	16.9%	9.7%	24.9%

Note: number of animals in each breed group shown in brackets
There were no other reciprocal crosses involving *B. taurus* breeds in this experiment
Source: Tawonezvi et al. (1988b)

available genotypes to suit their particular requirements within a certain environment.

Crossbred cows are frequently mated to bulls of a third breed to produce a terminal cross for slaughter. This is known as three-breed terminal crossing; a system that requires three separate mating herds (unless artificial insemination is used) and three breeds of bull (Fig 27). Furthermore, proper identification and adequate records of each individual animal are required; otherwise animals may not be allocated to the correct breeding group.

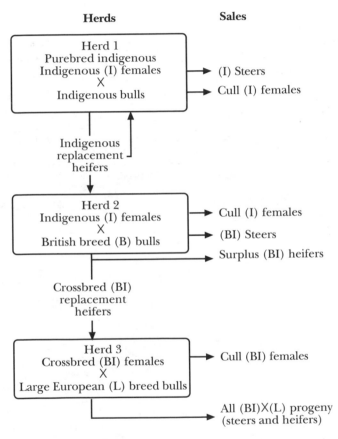

Fig 27   *Three-breed terminal cross*

Records of cows and calves

Efficient management of a herd requires accurate records of breeding performance. Stockowners should record the number or name of the cow, the date on which the bull was introduced to the herd (or date of insemination if mated individually or by AI), the date of calving, the number of days between successive calvings, the sex of the calf, date of weaning and any additional information such as whether it is the cow's first calving, whether she had trouble calving, or if the calf died. The information should be kept on a record card (Table 25). Some stock-owners have more elaborate systems with individual cards for each cow, but the important point is to keep records up to date. The information will identify cows that are performing well and those that should be culled.

Table 25   Record card for cows and calves in a beef herd

Name/ no. of cow	Name/ no. of bull + date entered herd	Date of birth of calf	Parity	Calving interval	No. of calf	Sex of calf	Date of weaning	Obser-vations
99012	99100 01.02.03	05.01.04	1	383	04001	M	05.08.04	Dystokia
			2		04002	F		

6 Reproduction and fertility

Differences in calving rate account for at least two-thirds of the variation between herds in the amount of beef produced per breeding cow per year. Even under ideal conditions with healthy fertile cows and an adequate number of active fertile bulls (100 per cent oestrus detection and fertile semen), calving rates of 100 per cent are unlikely. Only 60–70 per cent of services or inseminations result in the birth of a calf, due to conception failures and embryonic deaths. (See *Livestock Behaviour, Management and Welfare* in this series for more information on fertility.)

Fertility in the male

The reproductive efficiency of a bull has a large effect on the profitability of beef production – much greater than that of growth trait and carcass quality. It depends on: a) production of adequate quantities of fertile semen; b) high libido to ensure he will actively seek and mate with cows in oestrus; and c) ability to mount and deposit semen in the reproductive tract of the female.

Although the health and semen quality of bulls used for artificial insemination are continually monitored, the fertility of bulls used for natural service is rarely investigated. Physical examination of bulls, observation of their activities and the keeping of simple records may be used to detect infertile and sub-fertile bulls, which should then be culled. For example, if a large number of cows repeatedly show oestrus in spite of being seen with the bull while on heat, then that bull should be assumed to be sub-fertile or infertile. It could also mean that the bull has a venereal infection such as campylobacteriosis (vibriosis) and the bull's semen should be analysed.

Fertility in the female

The reproductive efficiency of a cow is determined by the ability to conceive and produce viable calves. It is measured as: a) calving rate, i.e. the number of calves born per year per 100 cows exposed to bulls (appropriate where controlled mating seasons of restricted length are practised); and b) calving interval, i.e. the time between successive calvings (used to assess efficiency in multipurpose and communally grazed herds where cows are mated throughout the year). The two measures are related. Achievement of a calving index of 100 per cent depends on a calving interval of 365 days or less. A calving interval of 16 months (486 days) leads to a calving rate of 75 per cent while a calving index of 50 per cent is associated with a calving interval of 24 months. Variation in calving interval depends almost entirely on the time between calving and successful conception (conception interval), since the gestation period normally varies between 280 and 285 days (282 to 290 days for Zebus). For a calving interval of 365 days, the conception interval should not exceed 83 days.

Breeding season

The time and length of the breeding season depends on the objectives of the cattle owner. The owners of multi-purpose herds may wish their cows to calve throughout the year to provide a continual supply of milk. If beef or calves are the major product of the herd, then a controlled breeding programme based on a limited breeding period has several advantages:

- the calving season can be planned to take advantage of seasonal changes in the availability and nutritional value of grazing or the availability of crop residues or to fit in with other farming operations including draught work;
- since all cows are at a similar stage of the reproductive cycle at the same time, supplementary feed is only given to the herd when it is really needed;
- bull performance may be readily monitored; and
- infertile and sub-fertile cows may be identified either at the end of the calving season or, preferably, by pregnancy diagnosis three months after the end of the bulling period. Culling infertile cows as soon as they can be identified will lead to an increase in calving rate.

If the breeding season is restricted, calving should be timed to make best use of the cheapest, best quality feed available (usually green grazing). Ideally, calves should be born four to six weeks before an adequate supply of green grass may be expected. This ensures that calves are large enough to use the potential high milk yields of cows grazing on young green grass. Cows calving at this time are also more likely to gain sufficient weight and condition and to re-conceive within 90 days after calving.

Oestrus and ovulation

During oestrus, a cow or heifer will stand to be mated by the bull. Oestrus occurs at approximately 21-day intervals and lasts for between 3 and 22 hours. The duration is shorter in *Bos indicus* than in *Bos taurus*. In the tropics, short oestrus periods are common during the hottest time of the year and often take place at night. Ovulation is the release into the fallopian tube of a mature ovum that may be fertilised, and this occurs 6–8 hours after the end of oestrus. Ovulation and oestrus do not occur in heifers before puberty or during the period of lactation anoestrus after calving. 'Silent' ovulations (not accompanied by oestrous behaviour) can occur in suckling cows. Identifying cows in oestrus is important so that animals may be hand served (i.e. the bull is brought to the cow) or inseminated at the time they are most likely to conceive. In addition, the herdsman may be alerted to the possibility of an infertile or sub-fertile bull.

Signs of oestrus

The most reliable indication of oestrus is that the cow or heifer will stand to be mounted by a bull or another cow. The female in oestrus may also try to mount other cows. Signs that the cow has been mounted (e.g. dirty rump and flanks and ruffled hair on the tail head) are further signs of oestrus. A clear string of mucus often hangs from the vulva and may adhere to the tail. The lips of the vulva may be swollen and a darker red than usual. (See *Livestock Behaviour, Management and Welfare* in this series for more information.)

Puberty and growth

Puberty in females is the time at which oestrus accompanied by ovulation first occurs. The age at puberty is important, because it determines the length of the non-productive rearing period and, indirectly, the lifetime production of the animal. Age is not the only factor that determines the attainment of puberty; in fact, body weight is more important. Heifers of the large European breeds (e.g. Charolais) are often heavier and younger at puberty than smaller breeds. *Bos taurus* animals reach puberty at 35 per cent and *Bos indicus* at 60 per cent of mature body weight. There is a genetically determined weight at which puberty will occur in each individual, and under-nutrition increases the time taken to attain this.

Fig 28 shows that when the weights of two-year-old Afrikaner cows are the result of different levels of nutrition, the proportion that conceive is related to body weight. However, there is no evidence that under-

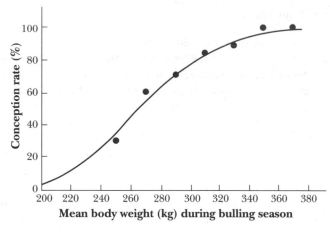

Fig 28 *Relationship between conception rate and body weight of two-year-old Afrikaner heifers at mating. Because conception and calving are widely separated in time only the successful conceptions are measured in terms of calving rate (Richardson, 1983)*

nutrition in early life influences subsequent reproductive performance once puberty has been achieved following restoration of an adequate diet.

Conception by lactating cows

Involution of the uterus (returning to its non-pregnant condition) has to occur before the cow can conceive again. The process takes about 30 days – less in suckling cows and first-calving animals – although involution may be delayed following dystokia (difficult calving) or retention of the placenta.

Prolonged lactation anoestrus in the tropics is usually the result of under-nutrition. The first oestrus after calving occurs ten days earlier in cows that gain weight both before and after calving than among cows that lose weight during this time. Nutritional status before calving is probably more important than post-calving weight changes in determining the length of the postpartum anoestrus. In both temperate regions and the tropics, post calving anoestrus is shorter in cows that are heavy immediately after calving than in cows of a poor nutritional condition.

The sucking stimulus of a calf also delays the onset of ovarian activity after calving. This effect can be reduced in three ways. First, by permanent weaning of calves shortly after birth and rearing them artificially. In Nigeria, weaning the calves of Bunaji cows at three days old reduced the mean interval from calving to conception to 73 days, compared with 233 days when cows suckled their calves normally. However, this is expensive and impractical in beef herds, especially in the tropics, because calves weaned so early will only survive if fed milk or milk substitute by bottle or bucket and/or given a diet that contains a high proportion of concentrates (Zebu calves are notoriously difficult to feed from a bottle or bucket).

Second, calves can be weaned temporarily for eight days just before the bulling season. When calves were prevented from sucking (by means of nose plates) at 50–58 days after calving, 55 per cent of cows showed oestrus by 60 days postpartum, compared with only 30 per cent for cows that suckled their calves continuously. If calves have access to concentrates during temporary weaning, their growth will not be adversely affected. The use of nose plates instead of separating the calves reduces stress for both cows and calves and they will resume normal suckling when these are removed. Third, preventing suckling at night can increase the proportion of cows that exhibit oestrus by 70 days postpartum to 85 per cent, compared with 13 per cent for those that were allowed to suckle at night. Night separation is traditional in many parts of Africa where cows are partially milked and partially suckled.

In multi-purpose herds, draught work may increase the time from calving to first oestrus. Working for four hours per day four days a week was shown to delay the onset of oestrus by 122 days. Different breeds also show different durations of postpartum anoestrus; for example 70 days for Mashona cows and 102 days for Afrikaners. A decrease in the length of the postpartum anoestrus should lead to a decrease in the calving interval and to an increase in calving rate.

Ability to conceive and maintain pregnancy

Maximising the chances of a successful pregnancy at each oestrus will ensure the highest possible calving rate. A high proportion of cows in oestrus must be detected and either served by a bull or artificially inseminated. If cows and bulls graze together (natural service), one active fertile bull is required for every 25–30 cows. The number of bulls should be increased in areas where there is a hilly landscape, tall grass or dense bush. Natural service is the most practical method to use when herds graze large paddocks. It also enhances the probability of conception in breeds having a short duration and/or mainly night oestrus. Stockmen must be trained to identify cows in oestrus if a bull is required to serve individual cows (hand service) or if artificial insemination is used.

Although approximately 85 per cent of ova released are fertilized, 30–40 per cent of embryos are lost by 40 days after insemination. Ensuring maximum embryo survival involves giving cows a high plane of nutrition (150 per cent of maintenance requirements) before and during ovulation. However, supplementary feed for cows on range or highly productive pastures are not required during early pregnancy, since a high plane of nutrition (especially a high protein diet) at this stage may be detrimental to embryo survival. Cows require a high energy intake at around 35–45 days after insemination to prevent embryo loss at final implantation stage.

The risk of foetal loss due to infectious disease must also be minimised. Several diseases (brucellosis, vibriosis or campylobacteriosis, Rift Valley fever and leptospirosis) cause abortion, but these can be prevented by routine vaccination of heifers at the appropriate age. If annual vaccination of cows is required, this is done at least six weeks before mating (see *Animal Health* in this series). Maintaining a closed herd and using artificial insemination can prevent the spread of venereal diseases (e.g. trichomonosis), which can cause abortion.

Other factors affecting calving rate

Heavy stocking rates on rangeland lead to reduced energy intake and lower the individual weight of cows and the calving rate. For example, mean calving rates in south-western Zimbabwe over four years were 52.7 per cent and 69.1 per cent when breeding herds were stocked at 0.27 and 0.12 cows/ha respectively. In regions deficient in protein or phosphorus (or both), appropriate supplementation leads to substantial increases in calving rate (Table 26).

Table 26   Mean calving rates (%) of Mashona cows over six years on rangeland in Zimbabwe

	Control	Groundnut cake 900g/day[1]
No phosphorus supplement	56.7	72.2
With phosphorus supplement[2]	61.7	76.7

1 During period 15 May to 15 November (dry season)
2 Phosphorus supplement and salt *ad libitum* throughout the year

The plane of nutrition and, therefore, body weight during pregnancy has a major influence on post-calving live weight and subsequent reconception (Fig 29). In addition, a greater percentage of Mashona than Afrikaner cows conceived at the same weight, implying that stockowners should keep the breed or strain that is most fertile in a specific environment.

Calving rates also tend to be reduced when cows are working. For example, a group of cows were given grass hay *ad libitum* as their only feed. In the cows that worked (4 hours per day, 4 days per week), only 6 per cent conceived by 200 days postpartum, compared with 47 per cent of the

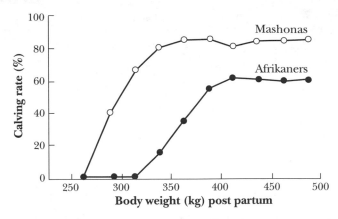

Fig 29 *Calving rate of Afrikaner and Mashona cows according to postpartum body weight (Holness et al., 1980)*

non-working cows. When the cows were given a supplement of 3 kg concentrates per day, the same work pattern reduced the calving rate from 76 to 40 per cent.

Condition scoring

Condition scoring compares animals on the basis of their relative fatness and is a useful measure of cattle body weight, particularly for small-scale stockowners without access to cattle scales. Although different condition scoring measures exist, the method is the same, with low scores indicating thin animals and high scores given to excessively fat animals. Fat cover is assessed by gripping the side of the animal halfway between the hook and the last rib (Fig 30). The thumb is used to feel the amount of fat over the transverse processes (Fig 31). The method developed by the International Livestock Research Institute (ILRI) for *Bos indicus* cattle includes a visual assessment of different parts of the animal and notes a lack of muscle in addition to fat cover. Under this system, cattle are allocated to one of nine categories:

1. Animal is emaciated.
2. Spine (dorsal processes) prominent and transverse processes feel sharp to the touch, with no detectable fat cover (Fig 32).
3. Individual dorsal spines are pointed to the touch. Hooks, pins, tail head and ribs are prominent. Transverse processes are visible, usually individually.
4. Ribs, hooks and pins are clearly visible. Muscle mass between hooks and pins slightly concave. Slightly more flesh over transverse processes than in point 3 above.

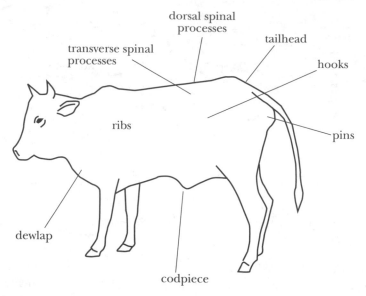

Fig 30 *Points at which cattle are examined to establish body condition (Chesworth, 1992)*

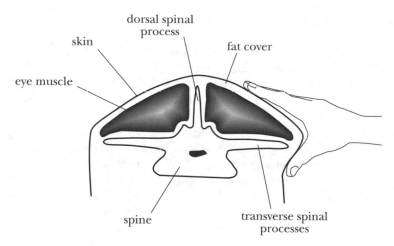

Fig 31 *Assessment of fat cover (Chesworth, 1992)*

5. Ribs usually visible; little fat cover; dorsal spines barely visible.
6. Animal smooth and well covered; dorsal spines cannot be seen but are easily felt.
7. Animal smooth and well covered; fat deposits are not marked. Dorsal spines can be felt with firm pressure, but are rounded rather than sharp (Fig 33).

Fig 32   *A cow scoring 2 on the condition scale (Pullen, 1978)*

Fig 33   *A cow scoring 7 on the above scale (Pullen, 1978)*

8. Fat cover in critical areas can be felt easily; transverse processes cannot be seen or felt.
9. Heavy deposits of fat clearly visible on tail head, dewlap and codpiece; ribs, hooks and pins fully covered and cannot be felt even with firm pressure.

A condition score of 5 or 6 on the above scale at calving is probably the optimum to ensure efficient conception rates. Although supplementary feeding may improve calving rate, the response to a high plane of nutrition is least in cows in very poor or very good condition and is most marked in cows of condition score 1 to 3 on the above scale.

7 Calf production

A high rate of pre-weaning mortality in calves is one of the main causes of low off-take for slaughter in pastoralist herds. Animals that are small for their age and breed at weaning will take longer to reach slaughter weight and will consume more feed than calves that are well grown at this stage. When calves are young, they use metabolisable energy for growth more efficiently than when they are older. Calf management strategies should therefore aim to maximise pre-weaning survival and promote an optimal growth rate for the production system.

Body weight at birth and calf viability

The optimum weight of a calf at birth is one close to the mean for the breed, since both very large and very small birth weight calves have lower survival rates from birth to weaning. The death of very large calves usually occurs during or shortly after birth and is connected to dystokia. During a study of the productivity of different breed types in Zimbabwe, one-third of all perinatal mortality was due to stillbirth as a result of dystokia. The incidence of dystokia appears to be related to body weight at birth and is higher among first calving heifers than older cows (Table 27).

Indigenous tropical breeds tend to produce relatively small calves and dystokia is rare. It is more common in large European breeds (e.g. Charolais) and in crossbred calves sired by these breeds. There are exceptions, however; for example, indigenous Zimbabwean cows (Mashona and Nkone) gave birth to Charolais cross calves with very little dystokia, even though the crossbred calves were heavier than purebred ones. In particular, Nkone cows experienced virtually no calving problems, irrespective of which breed sired their calves.

The incidence of dystokia is higher when cows are carrying male calves, since these tend to be larger and heavier at birth than female calves. If cows are already well fed, increasing the plane of nutrition during

Table 27 Mean body weights at birth (kg) and the incidence of dystokia[1] (in brackets) of calves from first-calving heifers according to breed of sire and dam

Breed of sire	Breed of dam				
	Afrikaner	Mashona	Nkone	Sussex	Charolais
Afrikaner	29.0 (4.5)	24.6 (5.3)	28.3 (3.0)	35.8 (12.9)	
Mashona	27.9 (9.1)	22.1 (1.8)			
Nkone	27.2 (0.0)	26.2 (0.0)			
Sussex	33.1 (18.6)	25.9 (14.3)	28.6 (2.8)	34.5 (9.6)	
Charolais	36.7 (35.0)	28.5 (9.1)	31.6 (0.0)	37.0 (32.5)	40.1 (52.3)

1 Number of calves assisted at birth/number of calvings x 100
Source: Ward et al. (1978)

pregnancy can lead to dystokia because the calves are likely to be heavier at birth. However, when cattle are kept in traditional production systems and on rangeland in Africa, the last third of pregnancy often coincides with the latter part of the dry season and under-nutrition of the in-calf cows leads to low birth weight calves. Under these conditions, pre-weaning mortality increases as calf body weight at birth declines below a genetically determined threshold. Mortality associated with low birth weights occurs throughout the pre-weaning period; for example, the cumulative mortality of N'Dama calves increased progressively with age from birth to 120 days. In addition, as weight at birth declined below 0.9 of the mean, the cumulative mortality to all ages increased substantially (Table 28).

Table 28 Pre-weaning mortality amongst N'Dama calves in traditionally managed herds in the Gambia

Body weight group at birth	Body weight at birth (kg)	Cumulative calf mortality			
		Day 30	Day 60	Day 90	Day 120
Low	< 14.1	3.6	7.0	10.7	13.8
Average	14.1–17.3	0.9	2.7	4.6	6.3
High	> 17.3	0.3	1.4	2.6	5.0

Source: Agyemang (1992)

Under-nutrition during late pregnancy leads to low yields of colostrum and milk and to poor maternal behaviour. Undersized and weak calves also have difficulty accessing the udders of their dams and, if they receive insufficient milk, they are less able to cope with adverse environmental conditions (e.g. heavy rain or extremes of ambient temperature). Calves that do not obtain sufficient colostrum may have inadequate protection from pathogens. Mortality rates associated with the birth of small weak calves may be reduced by:

- feeding supplementary feed to pregnant cows or reserving the best grazing for them;
- close supervision of cows at calving to ensure that newborn calves obtain sufficient colostrum and milk;
- providing shelter to protect calves from excessive heat and cold;
- preventing the build-up of pathogens by moving calves to clean sites or disinfecting static ones; and
- separating the calves from their dams at night to protect them from trampling by mature cattle (Fig 34).

Fig 34   *Tethered Fulani calves on the Jos Plateau in Nigeria*

Calf growth and nutrition

Newborn calves consume milk only, but as they grow they increase their intake of solid feed. Consumption of both milk and solid feed (usually grass) influences the rate of calf growth. Stocking rate is a major factor affecting the plane of nutrition and the performance of both cows and calves. In an experiment carried out in Zimbabwe, calves of cows subjected to a heavy stocking rate (0.28 cows/ha) were lighter at birth and weaning, consumed less milk and had a higher mortality than the calves of lightly stocked cows (0.115 cows/ha) (Table 29). Pre-weaning growth rate of calves increases with an increase in the amount of milk consumed.

Table 29   Effect of different stocking rates on calf production parameters

Production parameters	Stocking rate (cows/ha)	
	0.28	**0.115**
Calf body weight at birth (kg)	28.8	31.2
Calf body weight at 150 days (kg)	107.8	135.5
Calf body weight at weaning (270 days) (kg)	134.2	176.2
Total milk consumption birth to 150 days (kg)	548.0	752.0
Pre-weaning calf mortality (%)	8.6	4.5

Source: Richardson and Khaka (1981)

However, the relation is curvilinear; the response in terms of additional gain per kg extra milk consumed decreases as the amount of milk consumed increases (Fig 35). There are three reasons for this. First, if solid feed such as grass is freely available, then solid feed intake decreases as milk consumption increases. Second, the digestibility of milk decreases as the amount consumed increases. Third, as calves become bigger and heavier, their maintenance expenditure increases and the energy requirement per unit of gain increases.

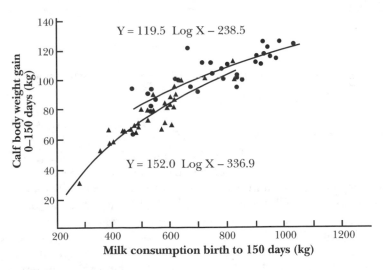

Fig 35   *Milk consumed by calves and their body weight increase*
Top line and circles = 0.115 cows/ha; lower line and triangles = 0.28 cows/ha;
Y is total calf weight gain between birth and 150 days of age; X is total milk consumed over
the same period (Richardson and Khaka, 1981)

This relationship has an important practical implication in the tropics, where cows are often expected to provide milk for human consumption in addition to suckling a calf. Taking milk for human use has a relatively small effect on calf growth rate, so long as the calf is able to consume sufficient milk. However, taking too much milk will adversely affect calf growth (Fig 36).

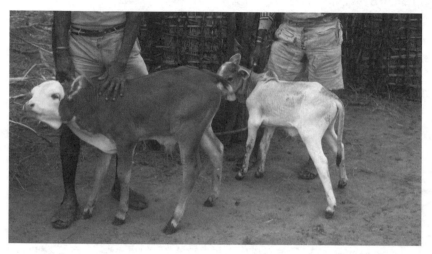

Fig 36   *Two calves in Tanzania of the same breed and age. The one on the left had all its dam's milk, while the one on the right had only half and the remainder was used for human consumption*

The amount of milk needed for a calf to grow adequately depends on its breed and its body size at birth. In a Fulani calf weighing around 22 kg at birth, this would be approximately 550 kg during the first 150 days (around 3 litres per day or two thirds of the cow's production). Calf body weight gains in the N'Dama have been measured as 205 g/day when the dams were not milked and 147 g/day when they were milked once daily. In this study, milking had little effect on calf mortality (4.3 per cent when cows were not milked and 6.5 per cent when they were). The evidence suggests that low milk intake is associated with increased calf mortality only when calves are relatively small at birth, unless their milk consumption is very low (< 2 kg/day) and their intake of solid feed is also restricted. Among calves consuming the same amount of milk, those grazing pasture where the herbage is sparse due to heavy stocking will gain less body weight than those that are lightly stocked with abundant grass.

Creep feeding is a means of providing feed to the calves alone by constructing an enclosure with openings of a height and width that will allow calves to pass but keep larger animals out. Creep feeds are usually concentrates, although high quality forages may be given. Giving a creep feed based on concentrates can increase body weight at weaning by up to 45 kg. However, the response is greatest among calves that are under-nourished and the extra gain resulting from creep feeding of well-fed calves is small and probably does not justify the cost of the feed. Creep feed is cost-effective during a drought, when rangeland is overstocked, or when calves are born late in the grass-growing season. In multipurpose herds, creep feeding of by-products (e.g. bran or rice polishings) will partially offset the adverse effects of milking on calf growth.

Weaning

In traditionally managed herds, calves are usually weaned naturally when the cow dries up at the end of her normal lactation period (7–12 months after calving). In commercial herds, calves are normally weaned earlier. Weaning can be managed by physically separating cows and calves. The calves may be confined in a pen or moved to a distant paddock so that dams and offspring cannot hear one another. Alternatively, nose plates can be used to prevent suckling, while allowing cows and calves the comfort of each other's presence.

When a cow is weaned, her energy expenditure is reduced and her body reserves of energy and protein and body weight will increase. This may lead to better conception rates during the following breeding season if she is given a low plane of nutrition (Table 30). In addition, a 6–8 week dry period restores udder tissue and ensures adequate milk yields during the subsequent lactation.

As would be expected, when comparing calves of the same age, those weaned later tend to be heavier (Table 30). The beneficial effect of late weaning is greater when the cow has a higher plane of nutrition (and calves have access to their dam's entire milk supply). Consequently, cows whose calves are weaned late produce a greater weight of weaned calf per annum than those weaned early, and this advantage increases with a higher plane of nutrition.

Calves can be weaned early and still achieve a good mature weight if they are given a diet containing at least 13 per cent crude protein. For example, calves weaned at 30 days and given a diet containing 30 per cent roughage and 70 per cent concentrates *ad libitum* while kept in pens achieved the same body weight at 210 days as calves weaned at 210 days reared on rangeland with access to their dams' full milk yield. The early weaned calves consumed 411 kg of concentrates/head. Such early weaning is normally only practised in dairy herds, where milk is more valuable for

Table 30   Effects of cow plane of nutrition and calf age at weaning on calving rate and calf production

| | Plane of nutrition | | |
| | Low | Medium | High |
	Calving rate (%)	Calving rate (%)	Calving rate (%)
Cows whose calves were weaned at 150 days	73.0 (72.9)	89.5 (87.5)	88.8 (86.4)
Cows whose calves were weaned at 240 days	68.2 (63.6)	86.5 (82.7)	97.7 (97.7)
	Mean calf body weight at 240 days (kg)		
Calves weaned at 150 days	158.7	160.4	169.1
Calves weaned at 240 days	167.8	169.2	184.0
	Mean weight of calf produced per cow per year (Weaning % x mean calf weight at 240 days)		
Calves weaned at 150 days	116.0	140.0	146.0
Calves weaned at 240 days	107.0	140.0	180.0

Weaning rates (calves weaned/100 cows mated) given in brackets
Source: Richardson et al. (1979)

human use than for feeding calves and when large quantities of concentrates are available.

Bull calves and surplus heifers from dairy herds can be raised for beef production; however, such a system is likely to be uneconomic in developing countries in Africa, the Caribbean and Pacific.

Castration

Calves should be castrated as young as possible (preferably before they reach three months) since older calves will experience a greater shock. There are three main methods:
1. Knife. This is the surest method, since the testicles are removed completely. It can be done at any age, although an anaesthetic should be used when castrating animals older than six months.
2. Burdizzo. This method is best suited to calves of 2–3 months and involves severing the spermatic cords without cutting the scrotum. Each cord should be severed separately but may be cut twice (Fig 37).

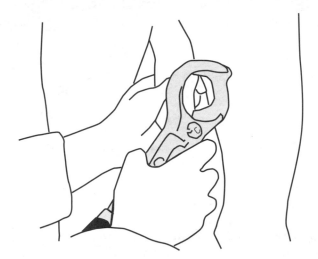

Fig 37 *Clamping burdizzo pincers to the scrotum of a bull calf*

3. Elastrator. This method involves placing a tight rubber band around the scrotum. The method must be used before the calf is a week old. Both testicles must be completely encircled by the ring, which should be placed very close to the body.

Further information can be found in Forse (1999). The effect of castration on growth and its importance as part of a livestock improvement programme are discussed in Chapter 4.

Dehorning

Horned cattle are likely to injure one another, especially when confined, and scars from horn wounds reduce the value of the hide. Consequently, some marketing organisations pay a bonus for dehorned cattle. However, if predators (e.g. leopards) are likely to attack the young calves, it may be wise to retain the cows' horns. Dehorning should be done within a month of birth and as soon as the horn bud can be felt. The process involves cauterising the horn bud and surrounding skin using a specially shaped dehorning iron, which is heated to a dull glow (Fig 38). Large horns may be removed by using a guillotine or saw. Alternatively, elastrator rings applied tightly to the base of a horn will cause it to fall off.

Identification

Identifying individuals and recording their performance is an essential part of herd management and enables superior stock to be selected for

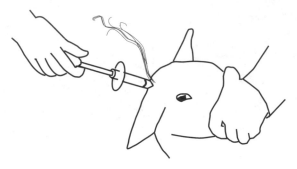

Fig 38   *Dehorning a calf*

breeding. Calves should be identified shortly after birth and their parentage recorded. African cattle have a wide range of colour patterns and horn shapes, and good herdsmen are able to accurately describe an individual, especially in the local language. However, these descriptions are not easy to record, especially by extension or animal health officers. Marking cattle with a system of numbers and letters is a useful alternative. The normal convention is to use a prefix to denote year of birth. For example, 03001 or D001 would indicate the first calf born in 2003, while 04002 or E002 would be the second calf of 2004.

Individual identification numbers can be applied to the animal by hot iron branding, tattooing (Fig 39), ear notching or fixing plastic ear tags (Fig 40). Good hot brands are permanent and may be read from a distance. However, cattle cannot be branded until they are over one year old because the skin is rather thin. Hot branding is also painful for the animal and damages the hide. With tattooing, an applicator forces ink under the skin of the ear. Tattoos are permanent but cannot be read unless the animal is caught or restrained. With ear notching, the ear is cut according to a code. The marks are fairly permanent, but the numbers are

Fig 39   *An ear tattoo*

74

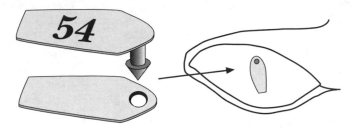

Fig 40   *An ear tag*

limited to a maximum of 300. Plastic ear tags are easy to apply and can be marked with permanent ink. They can be read from a distance and groups of animals can be identified by different colours. Unfortunately, the tags are easily lost and should be backed up by tattoos.

8 Growing and fattening

The aim of fattening (or finishing) beef cattle during the final period before slaughter is to: a) increase carcass weight, fatness and grade and improve carcass value; b) reduce age at slaughter and increase turnover; and c) take advantage of expected high prices which result from seasonal shortages of cattle that are suitable for slaughter.

During the fattening period, stockowners aim to increase the rate of weight gain. This can be achieved by different methods and the one chosen depends on: a) the live weight gain required before slaughter; b) the time available to achieve this gain; and c) the feed and other resources available and their cost in relation to the increase in carcass value.

The ideal carcass

The characteristics of the 'ideal' beef carcass depend on the perception of the consumer. For the western-type customer, it should contain a high proportion of muscle relative to bone but should not be excessively fat. For this market, the optimum carcass weight at slaughter varies with the genotype and is between 49 and 55 per cent of the peak weight attained by mature breeding cows during the year (e.g. for a cow attaining a peak weight of c. 450 kg, the ideal carcass weight of the progeny is c. 220–250 kg). To achieve this, live weight at slaughter should be 400–450 kg. The optimum slaughter weight of crossbred animals would be halfway between those of the two parent breeds. As heifers have a higher proportion of body fat than steers of the same weight, their ideal slaughter weight is about 15 per cent less than that of steers of the same breed. Amongst animals of the same weight and genotype, yearlings have a higher proportion of body fat than three-year-olds; consequently the ideal slaughter weight of a yearling is 12 per cent less than that of a three-year-old. This is because yearlings are growing faster than older animals of the same weight and so are depositing more fat.

It is not uncommon in the tropics for beef animals to be slaughtered at sub-optimal weights, particularly during periods of low rainfall when forage is in short supply or when stockowners wish to take immediate advantage of high prices, for example during holidays and festivals. The concept of target weights is a useful planning and management aid to ensure that slaughter cattle and replacement heifers attain the optimum weight at the right time. Targets are set for each phase of the animal's life and usually coincide with seasonal changes in nutritional status (Table 31). Both the environment and the production system chosen will modify the targets at each stage. The approach has the advantage of providing a yardstick for continual evaluation of performance and re-assessment of the feasibility of planned targets, which may have to be adjusted according to changing circumstances. If targets are not met and age at sale or slaughter cannot be increased, then expensive concentrate feed may be required to ensure that cattle reach a satisfactory weight. If slaughter prices and feed costs are known, it may be possible to work out if it is

Table 31   Target weights for Afrikaner, Sussex or Brahman cattle reared under different systems

	Natural grazing	Natural grazing + dry season protein[1]	Natural grazing + dry season protein + 350 kg cubes[2]	Natural grazing + dry season protein Feedlot at 15 months	Calves fed on creep feed Steers kept in feedlot after weaning
Age at slaughter (months)	43	31	27	19	>12
Final live weight (kg)	425	400	400	375	360
Live weight at 31 months (kg)	350	400[3]	–	–	–
Live weight at 19 months (kg)	240	290	320	–	–
Live weight at 7 months (kg)	140	180	200	210	240

Note: 210 days is the standard weaning age for beef cattle
1 0.5 kg/day of 50% crude protein concentrates during the dry season
2 350 kg of 16% crude protein concentrate during the early part of the rainy season
3 Some animals may reach slaughter weight before this age

cost-effective to feed concentrates. Providing concentrate feed can offset the effects of dry season weight loss and reduce age at slaughter. Conversely, heavy stocking rates can reduce growth rates and lead to an increase in the age at which the animals reach slaughter weight.

Improving growth rates on pasture

Growth rates on pasture can be improved by: a) applying nitrogen fertilizer to the pasture; b) growing legumes and seeded/improved grass pastures as forage; and c) supplementing the diet with concentrate feed. Decisions regarding these options depend on the local climate and soil and on the cost and availability of fertilizers and concentrates.

Nitrogen fertilizer

Applying nitrogenous fertilizer increases the yield and crude protein content of forage on natural and planted pasture and will be cost-effective in areas where annual rainfall exceeds 750 mm. Planted pastures generally give a better return (improved yield) than natural pastures, but the increase in yield varies with the species planted. In the Philippines, replacing native *Imperata cylindrica* pasture (a very poor pasture species) with planted *Brachiaria mutica* and adding 100 or 200 kg N/ha/year led to an increase in the rate of gain of two-year-old steers and allowed a higher stocking rate, leading to a three-fold increase in production per hectare (Table 32).

Table 32   Live weight gains, stocking rate and production per hectare on native *Imperata cylindrica* and planted pastures in the Philippines

Pasture	Stocking rate (steers/ha)	Live weight gain (kg/head/day)	Live weight gain (kg/ha/year)
Imperata cylindrica	1	0.27	100.0
Brachiaria mutica + 100 kg N/ha/year	2	0.36	260.0
Brachiaria mutica + 200 kg N/ha/year	3	0.28	310.8
Brachiaria mutica + Centrosema pubescens	2	0.42	305.4

Source: Butterworth (1985)

Legume-grass pastures

Many small-scale producers may not be able to afford nitrogenous fertilizer. Another option is to plant leguminous fodder species with the grass. Legumes have a higher crude protein content (17 per cent) than tropical grasses (7.7 per cent) and increase herbage yields and digestibility. The use of tropical legume–grass pastures has the potential to double or triple the live weight gain of steers per hectare. For example, in Zimbabwe, weaned steers grazing a mixed legume pasture for a year gained 205 kg compared with 117 kg for those grazing reverted arable land at a similar stocking rate (1.1–1.2 animals/ha). In the Philippines, sowing *Brachiaria mutica* with the legume *Centrosema pubescens* led to similar rates of gain and production/ha as an application of 100–200 kg N/ha/year (Table 32). However, this high level of production can only be sustained when the proportion of legume in the pasture is maintained by applying phosphate fertilizers at the start of the rains, and appropriate stocking rates are adopted.

Supplementing the diet with protein-rich concentrates

Limited amounts of protein-rich concentrates (16 per cent crude protein) can be given to grazing cattle to increase carcass weight and value or to reduce age at slaughter. For example, feeding 400 kg concentrates to grazing steers before slaughter gave similar increases in carcass weight irrespective of whether the animals were slaughtered at 33 or 44 months of age. Animals kept for an additional nine months, given no concentrates during the wet season and slaughtered early in the following wet season produced slightly heavier carcasses than those given concentrates prior to slaughter late in the previous wet season (Table 33). If prices are high early in the following wet season it may be beneficial to keep the animals longer and save on feed costs. However, keeping animals longer increases the herd size and stocking rate.

Supplementing the diet of growing cattle with concentrates is a cost-effective strategy when grass is plentiful, concentrates are relatively cheap and beef prices are high during the early or middle parts of the rainy season (Fig 41).

Pen and stall feeding (zero grazing)

In zero grazing systems, animals are confined to a small pen or stall and fodder is brought to them (Fig 42). The advantage of such a system is that confinement reduces the animal's energy expenditure and so increases the efficiency of feed conversion. The animal's manure can

Table 33 Live weight and carcass weight gains of steers weighing 270 kg at two years (grazing natural pasture)

Treatment (rainy season)	Age at slaughter (months)	Final live weight (kg)	Carcass weight (kg)	Carcass weight response to rainy season supplement (kg)
Grazing only	33	399.3	202.7	–
Grazing + 400 kg[1] concentrate (late season)	33	437.0	232.9	30.2
Grazing only	44	475.5	245.7	–
Grazing + 400 kg concentrate (early season)	44	515.5	277.8	32.1

All animals given a supplement of 0.5 kg cottonseed meal/day during the dry season
1 4 kg/day 16% crude protein concentrates for last 100 days before slaughter
Source: Grant (1977)

Fig 41 *Thin cattle on abundant grass sward – these cattle would benefit from a supplement of high-protein concentrate*

also be collected and applied to crops as fertilizer. The disadvantage is that the stockowner has to find a reliable source of good quality fodder for the animals. The main diets used to fatten beef cattle in zero grazing

Fig 42   *Crossbred steers being fed on a high-grain diet in Zimbabwe*

systems in the tropics are: a) molasses-based; b) based on crop residues and agro-industrial by-products; and c) harvested forage crops. Rations may also be based on high-grain diets (> 35 per cent grain) if surplus grain is available.

Molasses-based diets

Large quantities of molasses are produced in many parts of the tropics and form an alternative source of energy to grain. Molasses may be fed absorbed onto dried cane pith and this can be mixed with a protein–mineral–vitamin concentrate. Animals given a molasses-based diet have similar daily feed intakes to those offered a maize-based diet with 20 per cent roughage, although they need an additional three weeks to achieve the same carcass weight and they eat 19 per cent more feed.

Liquid molasses/urea diets have been used successfully for fattening cattle in Cuba. The mixture comprises 93.5 per cent final molasses, 2 per cent urea, 0.5 per cent salt and 4 per cent water. The animals should be given 1.5 kg/100 kg live weight of fresh forage such as Napier grass or whole maize plant and a protein concentrate supplying 80 g/100 kg live weight of a slow degradable protein (e.g. cottonseed meal). To prevent molasses toxicity, cattle entering the feedlot should be accustomed to the diet by restricting molasses intake to 1 kg/head on the first day and increasing the quantity by 0.5 kg/day until they achieve their *ad libitum* intakes. Over the same period, the amount of fresh forage offered should be reduced from *ad libitum* to 1.5 kg/100 kg live weight. The molasses troughs should be protected from direct sunlight to prevent the feed heating up and becoming less palatable.

Crop residues and by-products

Intensive poultry systems produce large amounts of poultry manure, which is a cheap source of true protein and non-protein nitrogen. Israeli Friesian bulls offered a diet comprising 35 per cent poultry manure and 55 per cent grain together with 1.5 kg hay/day gained 0.96 kg live weight and 0.53 kg carcass weight per day over 167 days. Manure from intensive pig systems has also been fed to intensively reared beef cattle. However, the risks of feeding animal waste products to other animals should be carefully evaluated, since diseases may be transmitted and the waste may contain contaminants such as antibiotics.

Dried citrus pulp may be used to replace some of the grain in a high-grain diet with little adverse effect on performance. It has a high fibre content but, because the lignin content is low, it is highly digestible and provides 12.6 MJ ME/kg DM. Cottonseed hulls may be used as roughage in feedlot diets.

Forage crops

Cultivated forage crops, including legumes such as berseem (*Trifolium alexandrium*) and leucaena (*Leucaena leucocephala*) and grasses such as Napier grass (*Pennisetum purpureum*) and maize (*Zea mays*), can be grown as forage crops for feeding to beef cattle. (More information can be found in *Forage Husbandry* in this series.)

High-grain diets

Animals fattened on high-grain diets convert the metabolisable energy of their feed to carcass gain very efficiently. Since efficiency is positively related to ME intake, the diet should be formulated to ensure maximum ME intake, which is achieved when the roughage content of the diet is about 20 per cent and the protein content about 12.5 per cent. If coarse-milled snapped corn (maize grain plus cob and husk) is mixed in the proportions 9:1 with a protein–mineral–vitamin mix (64 per cent crude protein), the roughage and protein contents will be approximately 20 and 13 per cent respectively. However, some *Bos indicus* breeds may develop laminitis (inflammation of the laminae in the feet) if the roughage content is less than 30 per cent. When animals have reached more than 40 per cent of their mature weight and are offered diets with 12.5 per cent protein, up to 45 per cent of dietary crude protein may be supplied by urea (the diet would then contain 2 per cent urea by weight) to reduce costs. For smaller animals, urea should not exceed 1 per cent of the diet and part of the grain should be replaced by natural protein (e.g. oilseed meals or legumes). However, grain is rarely available for feeding beef animals in developing countries (see Chapter 2).

Length of the fattening period and total amount of feed

Fattening of cattle is profitable only when the increase in carcass value exceeds the cost of the additional feed required. The growth of steers having an initial live weight of 290 kg and offered a diet with 20 per cent roughage and 12.5 per cent crude protein *ad libitum* is used as an example. Groups of ten steers were slaughtered at the start of the trial and at four-week intervals thereafter. As the feeding period increased, carcass weights increased, but the amount of additional carcass produced for each extra kg of feed decreased (Table 34). The amount of additional feed required to produce 1 kg of additional gain increases with the length of feeding period. This is a result of increasing maintenance expenditure and fat content of the carcass. As a result of their large size, cull cows require more than 16 kg feed to produce 1 kg extra gain even in the early stages of fattening when gaining more than 1 kg/day. Consequently, pen fattening of this type of animal is uneconomic and they should be finished on pasture.

Table 34 Amounts of feed eaten, carcass weights, additional gain per kg extra feed and the feed required for additional carcass weight gain

Days in feedlot	Total feed eaten (kg)	Final live weight (kg)	Carcass weight (kg)	Additional carcass weight per kg extra feed[1]	Feed per kg extra gain (kg)
0	0.0	289.0	14.4	–	–
28	237.3	331.3	167.9	0.106	9.48
56	586.7	382.6	203.9	0.095	10.58
84	884.9	416.9	230.4	0.085	11.74
112	1249.9	458.2	253.7	0.074	13.57
140	1592.7	501.4	283.5	0.063	15.89

1 This value was obtained by differentiating the quadratic function fitted to the data for carcass weight and cumulative feed intake
Source: Groenewald and Hopley (1976)

9 Drought

Livestock are the main source of livelihood in many parts of the semi-arid tropics, where rainfall is too scarce and unreliable for people to grow crops. Semi-arid and arid regions comprise 55 per cent of the land area of Africa and 57 per cent of African domestic ruminants are found in this region. In many parts of Africa where cattle are kept, drought years occur frequently – as often as three years in every ten. Cattle, sheep and goats are the animals of choice in drought-prone areas because they can survive and produce a reasonable yield in semi-arid conditions, but their performance will be reduced in dry years and large numbers may die when there is a prolonged drought.

Forage

Grass growth is highly dependent on rainfall and herbage dry matter production can vary as much as fourfold between years (Fig 43). Other factors, such as the distribution of rainfall during the season, also have a large effect on herbage growth (e.g. yields will be low when rainfall occurs late in the season). Periods without measurable rain can last as long as eleven months. When drought causes a scarcity of forage, grazing cattle will have a reduced energy intake and will experience moderate to severe weight loss, especially towards the end of the dry season. There will also be an increase in mortality and carcasses will be light and of low quality. In addition, conception rates will be substantially reduced.

To develop strategies to minimise the adverse effects of drought on the long-term productivity of cattle, we need to understand how forage availability and the live weight of different classes of animal vary over time and with rainfall. Scientists at the University of Cape Town have developed a computer model that simulates the relationships between livestock, vegetation and rainfall. Where there are distinct wet and dry

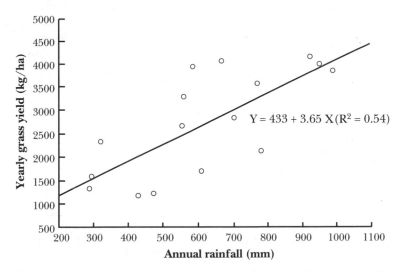

Fig 43   *The relationship between grass production (kg/ha/yr) and annual rainfall (mm) on a moderately fertile sandy loam. Trees and shrubs removed*

seasons, grass grows faster than cattle can eat it during the wet season, so herbage density increases. In the dry season, there is little or no grass growth and the density of standing forage decreases progressively as cattle graze. Because cattle graze selectively, the digestibility of available herbage also declines over time. Cow and calf weights increase even after herbage density has started to decline, although the decline starts earliest in the years when grass cover is least. During the first dry year, adverse effects on cow and calf weights, reproduction and survival may be relatively small (Table 35 and Fig 44).

However, in the second dry year, especially if the rains are late, grass growth may be even slower. Both cows and calves suffer substantial weight losses and more will die towards the end of the dry season. The adverse effects of a second drought year may be mitigated by reducing the number of animals, i.e. stocking density, when the probability of poor grass yields is foreseen. Figure 45 shows that by the time animals start to lose weight rapidly (week 36 in year 2), grass is already scarce. This indicates that during a drought, monitoring the vegetation may be a better aid to management than monitoring animal condition. Measuring cumulative rainfall for the current season and inspecting the grazing will help the stockowner decide to de-stock sufficiently early to prevent serious losses.

Table 35 Effect of stocking rate and drought on predicted conception rates and cow and calf survival

	Year 1 0.25 cows/ha	Year 2 0.25 cows/ha	Year 2 0.125 cows/ha
Rainfall (mm)	366	338	338
Conception rate	0.840	0.420	0.500
Cow mortality	0.010	0.450	0.017
Calf mortality	0.017	0.525	0.020

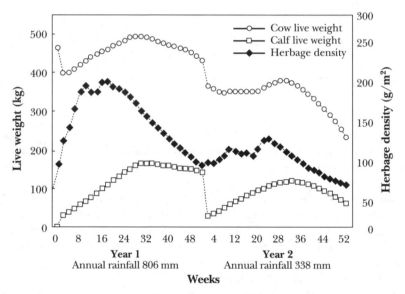

Fig 44 *Relationship between herbage density and cow and calf live weights over time (stocking rate 0.25 cows/ha)*

When deciding which animals to sell, stockowners should aim to retain the animals that will ensure rapid rebuilding of the herd (i.e. fertile breeding cows). Early disposal of the least productive animals makes scarce feed resources available for the rest of the herd. Calves older than six months may be weaned and sold and this will reduce the energy expenditure and weight loss of their dams. Oxen or steers do not need to be kept purely for working since cows may be used instead.

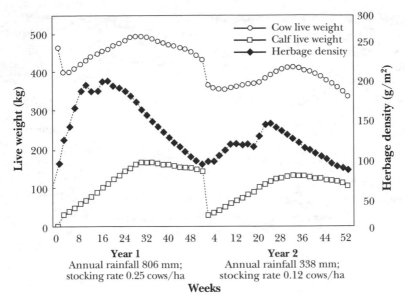

Fig 45 *Relationship between herbage density and cow and calf live weights over time*

Water

A dairy cow in a temperate climate will require 5 litres of water per 100 kg body weight per day. The water requirement of cattle in the tropics is much higher (around 10 litres per 100 kg per day). Most cattle need to be watered every day, although local breeds such as the Borana and the Boran (Fig 46) can go for three days without water.

When planning the best use of available grazing, stockowners should take account of the expected availability, quality and distribution of water. Many water points dry up during a drought and as the dry season advances, the distance between water points increases, forcing cattle to walk further each time they need to drink. This results in grass situated far from water being under-used while areas close to water are overgrazed. Cows should be herded to graze first around water points that are expected to fail, thereby conserving forage around the more reliable water sources. When forage is abundant, cattle drink daily and rarely graze more than 5 km from water. However, they can graze up to 20 km from a water point if herded and allowed to drink only every third day. If they walk slowly (< 5 km/h), the energy cost of walking will be low and they will not lose excess weight; neither will their calves. When suckling cows were watered every three days, those made to walk 20 km to and from water lost 75 kg during the season while those not herded and drinking

Fig 46   *Boran beef cattle in Zambia*

every day lost 64 kg. At seven months, their calves weighed 132 and 141 kg respectively.

In the Ethiopian Rift Valley, watering Borana cattle once every three days had little effect on mortality, calving rate or the weight of two-year-old steers, although calf live weight was greater with daily watering (Table 36). Cattle that are adapted to dry areas (e.g. Borana) can graze long distances from water and will re-hydrate quickly without suffering from water intoxication. Cattle from most other breeds should be discouraged from drinking too much too quickly if they have been deprived of

Table 36   **Drinking frequency and productivity of Borana cattle**

| | **Drinking frequency** | | |
	Once a day	Every second day	Every third day
Calving rate (no. calves per annum)	0.74	0.76	0.78
Calf weight at 210 days (kg)	139.60	130.80	125.50
Steer weight at 2 years (kg)	312.80	308.40	306.10
Dry season lactating cow weight loss (kg)	83.40	68.40	111.40

Source: Nicholson (1987)

water for more than a day. Watering lactating cows once in three days reduced their water consumption by 30 per cent compared with daily watering but pre-weaning calf growth was reduced by no more than 10 per cent and this difference was almost eliminated by the time the animals were two years old.

During a drought, much of the available water is salty. If it contains more than 10 g total soluble salts (TSS) per litre, and is unpalatable to humans, it is unsuitable for cattle. They will reduce their voluntary feed intake and productivity will suffer.

Carrying capacity

In Chapters 4 and 5 we have seen that heavy stocking rates tend to reduce the productivity of growing cattle (Tables 17 and 19). However, pastoralists are usually prepared to accept a reduction in production per animal if they can keep more animals, since this may maximise production per hectare. The number of animals kept on common land in KwaZulu, South Africa and productivity per animal has not decreased during the past 70 years, despite being greatly in excess of estimated or recommended carrying capacity (Tapson, 1993).

Herbage production varies widely between years and this variability is greatest when rainfall is less than 500 mm per annum. Production also varies within landscapes; forage production in key resource (wetter) areas such as *vleis* and *dhambos* (seasonally waterlogged depressions), deep alluvial soils and river banks can be as much as ten times that predicted by the FAO formula for recommended carrying capacity (see Chapter 2). This partly explains the substantial differences between predicted and observed carrying capacities in many areas. Where annual rainfall is below 500 mm and land is stocked according to the FAO formula, low forage yields and stock losses still occur in one or two years in ten, but losses can be prevented if animal numbers are reduced as soon as a shortage of forage is anticipated. On the other hand, very low stocking rates can waste much usable forage in years of above average rainfall.

Survival feeding

When there is virtually no grazing available (as occurs following consecutive seasons of very low rainfall or fire), the core herd of breeding animals must be given sufficient nutrients to keep them alive until the grass grows again. Cattle adapt to under-nutrition by reducing their maintenance expenditure. For example, when the body weight of 185 kg Boran steers was kept constant for 24 weeks by adjusting the amount of feed given in response to weight changes, the feed (with 10.5 MJ ME/kg DM) required to maintain weight decreased from 3.39 to 1.66 kg DM/day. The weight of the digestive tract, liver and kidneys also declined and, because they contribute substantially to an animal's basal metabolism, their reduction in size contributes to a reduced maintenance energy requirement.

Allowing animals to lose weight will lead to a further reduction in the amount of feed needed for their survival. When 440 kg non-pregnant dry Afrikaner cows were given 21 MJ ME/day (1.81 kg of a complete diet, containing 1.67 kg DM) for 32 weeks they lost 149 kg but remained healthy, and live weights stabilised after about 18 weeks (Fig 47). The diet given in this case contained 80 per cent concentrate, 20 per cent roughage and 16.9 per cent crude protein in the dry matter. As might be expected, in-calf and lactating cows need more than this to survive. Research in Australia has shown that if cows are to successfully rear a calf to 10 weeks of age, they should be given 46 MJ ME/day during the last 100 days of pregnancy and until the calves are weaned at 10 weeks old. This may be supplied by 4 kg/day of rolled sorghum grain or 4.8 kg/day of survival diet 1 or 2 (Table 37). If possible, suckling calves should have access to creep feed, such as bran or rolled sorghum grain mixed with 1 per cent limestone flour.

Survival rations based on bush meal (branches and twigs ground in a hammer mill) are not relevant to developing regions, because special

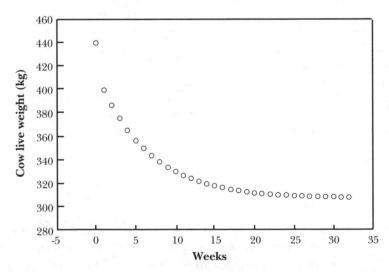

Fig 47   *Mean live weights of Afrikaner cows fed on 1.81 kg of a complete diet per day (Elliott et al., 1966)*

Table 37   Survival diets developed in Zimbabwe

	Survival diet 1 (%)	Survival diet 2 (%)
Maize grain	60.0	
Milled roughage	30.0	
Cottonseed cake	7.0	11.5
Urea	1.0	1.5
Limestone flour	1.0	
Salt	1.0	
Molasses/bagasse[1]		87.0
ME (MJ/kg DM)	9.6	9.6
Crude protein (%)	12.0	12.5

1 Dried sugar cane fibre

equipment and large amounts of power are required. If possible, cattle fed survival rations should be confined because walking increases weight loss. If good quality (not mouldy) roughage (e.g. hay, maize stover) is available locally, up to 60 per cent of survival rations can be based on this, but the total amount offered must increase with an increase in roughage content so that ME intake is adequate. If feed has to be brought in to a drought-stricken area, the transport costs per unit of ME are lower for concentrates due to their high energy value and high weight-to-bulk ratio. Because animals given very small quantities of feed may develop depraved appetites, stones and other debris must be removed from their pens and a hard salt lick and water *ad libitum* should be provided. Survival feeding is expensive, so only the minimum number of animals should be fed and those not required to rebuild the herd must be sold. The more animals that are sold when a severe shortage of forage is anticipated, the shorter the time for which survival rations must be provided. If food has to be purchased from outside the area, it is better to buy concentrates than roughage as a far greater weight of grain can be carried on a truck compared with hay. The grain also has a higher metabolisable energy content.

Breed and drought survival

When selecting the breed of cattle to keep, stockowners in drought-prone areas should focus on drought-tolerant breeds. One of the most impor-tant characteristics is the ability to walk long distances under high ambient temperatures. Not surprisingly, breeds native to the tropics are better adapted than British breeds; for example walking 25 km caused a greater

91

increase in respiration rate and rectal temperature in British (Hereford and Shorthorn) than in native (Afrikaner and Santa Gertrudis) steers. British breeds have longer hair and take shorter strides (thus use more energy) than tropical breeds. Interestingly, crossbred cattle seem better able to tolerate walking than purebred *Bos indicus* animals. The different breeds appear to have similar energy requirements for survival; however, because *Bos indicus* recycle more nitrogen to the rumen than *Bos taurus* when given low-protein roughages, they probably require less protein in drought rations (although this has not been tested experimentally with animals given very small quantities of feed).

Poisonous plants

Cattle are more likely to eat poisonous plants during a drought when there is little else available. Stockowners should therefore aim to graze their animals on areas affected by poisonous plants while the grazing is still green and to keep their animals away during the latter part of the dry season (see Chapter 2).

10 Marketing, transportation, slaughter and processing

At some time during the life of cattle in a herd that is partially or solely kept for the production of meat, the decision has to be made to slaughter the animals for human consumption. The reasons for doing this may not be entirely to produce meat but may be influenced by climate, social pressures or by economic considerations. If the animal is killed for local consumption then transportation and processing do not enter the equation, but if the beef is destined for export, then marketing, transportation and processing of the meat become important because they influence the economic success of the enterprise.

Marketing

The marketing of beef cattle covers the marketing of finished cattle for slaughter and the marketing of animals when they are moved from breeding areas to areas where they can be fattened. It also covers marketing of the meat product itself, both before and after processing (but this is beyond the scope of this book) and distress marketing of cattle in times of drought.

As discussed in Chapter 2, cattle in the tropics are kept by smallholders and traditional pastoralists and by ranchers who operate on a larger, commercial scale. Different types of producer will have different marketing objectives. Smallholders and pastoralists may sell a few quality animals to release cash for specific purposes or larger numbers of animals in poor condition in times of drought. In contrast, ranchers have an organised rearing and fattening programme aimed at producing finished animals for a specific market at a specific time. The way cattle are marketed will also vary considerably from country to country, depending on which types of production predominate.

In the nomadic pastoral sector, animals may be sold in local markets, to traders or to other producers for fattening. Attempts to take pastoralist cattle and fatten them intensively elsewhere (to standards suitable for export) have been generally unsuccessful, due mainly to the relatively high price of maize to beef and to unreliable supply of cattle. For example, a scheme set up in Nigeria to fatten cattle from the dry north and supply them to urban areas in the south failed due to problems of lack of supply of cattle and feed as well as a high incidence of disease (Fig 48).

The marketing of live cattle is normally controlled by networks of livestock traders, who tend to demand very large margins because they take the risk of losses while the animals are being transported and held prior to slaughter. The system normally works well and has proven much more successful than government marketing schemes.

Because of the length of time taken to breed, rear and finish an animal for beef, specialist beef production by smallholders tends to concentrate on one part of the production cycle, namely the finishing process. Such a scheme has been practised successfully in Malawi where smallholders in the south of the country fatten one or two cattle sourced from the cattle herds in the north. For this to be profitable there must be a sufficient margin between the price paid for immature stock and that earned for finished beef animals (see Table 13 on page 33). Buying an immature steer requires the small-scale farmer to make a large investment and take a big risk (if the animal dies his return will be zero) and many smallholders have no access to cash or credit facilities. The practice of fattening cattle that belong to other people (agisting) reduces both risk and capital outlay although the profit will be relatively small.

Two problems underlie cattle marketing in developing countries, especially in the more arid regions: a) variability in the supply of animals

Fig 48   *Empty pen at the Beef Fattening Centre at Mokwa in Nigeria*

suitable for slaughter; and b) variability in the prices paid. Many cattle marketing schemes in Africa have failed, at least partly because low prices paid to producers ensured that there was insufficient throughput to cover the overheads of the processing facilities.

Transportation and holding

Cattle may be moved long distances between their breeding areas and the final place of slaughter. On the way, they may be held in quarantine grounds to prevent the spread of disease or holding grounds prior to sale or slaughter. Both should have adequate feed and water. When holding pens are overcrowded, animals are likely to become stressed or injured and the quality of the carcass will be adversely affected. Washing the animals before putting them in a holding pen is beneficial, since it reduces the risk of disease and contamination of the carcass and it will minimise heat stress.

Animals may be trekked to market and stock herders must ensure the animals have sufficient feed and water on the way. They must also prevent their stock from damaging any crops they pass. Designated stock routes, which provide grazing and water and have veterinary inspection facilities en route, are used in some countries (e.g. Nigeria). Transportation by truck is becoming more common and avoids the problem of travelling through quarantine areas. However, transport by truck in hot climates can be extremely stressful for cattle. Drivers should avoid travelling in the middle of the day and going for long periods without watering the cattle. Vehicles passing from one region to another may need to be disinfected (Fig 49). Beef destined for export must be guaranteed free from disease, a process requiring veterinary inspection. (For more information on veterinary inspection see the *Animal Health* books and for information on transportation see *Livestock Behaviour, Management and Welfare* in this series.)

Transportation and the degree of stress can greatly affect the weight and quality of a beef carcass. Too much stress will lower the amount of glycogen in the muscle. If there is insufficient glycogen to produce about 1 per cent lactic acid by anaerobic breakdown after slaughter, the final pH of the muscle will not reach the required 5.5–5.6. This will interfere with the formation of bright red oxymyoglobin when the muscles are cut and exposed to the air. A large depletion of glycogen (due to underfeeding and/or excessive exercise) results in 'dark cutting' beef with a purplish-red hue. Beef of this type will not only be unattractive to the eye but will have a high pH (about 6.0), which may lead to the production of hydrogen sulphide by bacteria and green discolouration, and it will probably also be tough. Cattle trekked a long way to market therefore

Fig 49   *Vehicle in Malawi being disinfected to reduce the risk of spreading foot and mouth disease*

need to be rested and fed before slaughter. Animals that have been transported without adequate care or held in unsatisfactory holding pens may have bruised flesh or broken legs, both of which diminish the quality and value of the meat.

Slaughter

Village slaughter

Many animals in developing countries are slaughtered on the farm in conditions of less than optimal hygiene, where there is a risk of disease spreading to humans. A well-designed village slaughter area (Fig 50) will maintain hygienic conditions if a few simple rules are followed:
* only healthy animals should be killed;
* the slaughter slab should be located away from human habitation and effluent should not be allowed to run into water supplies;
* other livestock and dogs should be kept away from the slaughter area (ideally by means of a fence);
* the slab should have a smooth surface that is easy to wash and a soak-away should be provided for the dirty water;
* fresh water should be available for washing the carcass, butchery tools and slab;
* shade and shelter should be provided for a butcher's shop and/or a place in which to hang the dressed carcasses; and
* dung and inedible materials should be buried in a pit.

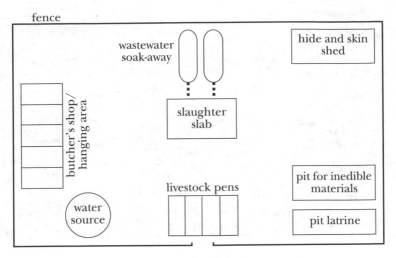

Fig 50   *Possible layout for a village slaughter area*

Equipment required to slaughter beef animals includes a poleaxe or captive bolt pistol (for stunning), a strong sharp knife, a meat saw, a hatchet, hooks for hanging the carcass and containers to collect the blood and internal organs.

Commercial slaughter

Commercial abattoirs serving a large area should be designed to maximise the welfare of the animals and minimise the risk of contamination of the meat by insects, parasites and micro-organisms. The carcass should never come into contact with the abattoir floor, and inedible by-products, such as gut contents, should be promptly removed from the slaughter area. Meat should be processed as quickly as possible. Fig 51 shows a well-designed commercial slaughterhouse.

Stunning

Cattle are usually killed by bleeding, which does not kill them immediately. Stunning them before bleeding will reduce animal suffering and enhance the safety of those involved in the slaughtering process. Cattle are normally stunned by a captive bolt pistol or a blow from a poleaxe. It is essential to stun the animal in the right place, ensuring that the medulla oblongata is not damaged. Damaging this part of the brain prevents the blood being pumped from the carcass and results in dark meat. The Jewish and Muslim religions do not allow animals to be stunned before they are bled.

Fig 51   *Slaughterhouse in Saudi Arabia*

Processing

After the animal is killed, the carcass must be handled carefully to ensure it is both acceptable to and safe for the consumer. Carcasses should be inspected immediately for signs of disease or parasites (e.g. the tapeworm *Taenia saginata*). Cooling the carcass immediately after slaughter will minimise contamination by bacteria. In areas without electricity, meat should be consumed as soon as possible after slaughter.

Carcass yield and quality

The carcass yield or dressing percentage of a beef animal is the weight of the carcass divided by the weight of the live animal expressed as a percentage. The dressing percentage increases as the animals get older and fatter. The dressing percentage of mature but thin animals may be as low as 45 per cent, but will rise to 60 per cent in well-finished, fat cattle. Fat animals therefore yield more useable meat per kilogram of live weight than thin ones.

Meat quality and desirability is influenced by colour, water holding capacity, texture and tenderness, and flavour (taste and odour). These characteristics are determined by the breed, sex, part of the animal from which the meat is taken (joint), age (young animals will produce more tender meat than mature ones), the way it has been fed, how it has been transported prior to slaughter, how it is held immediately before slaughter, the way it is slaughtered and the way it is stored after slaughter.

Meat storage

Beef becomes more tender when it is stored for a short period because of the effects of proteolytic enzymes (which start to digest the meat), but after a certain time the quality will begin to deteriorate. The higher the storage temperature, the faster the rate of deterioration. Beef can be preserved by the methods outlined in Table 38. Although freezing is probably the best method, a reliable source of electricity is unlikely to be available in rural areas in the tropics. A simpler method is to preserve the meat by drying and salting, which deprives potentially contaminating bacteria of water and therefore prevents them growing. The resulting product is known as charqui, biltong or pemmican. Meat preserved in this way should be cooked before eating to kill any remaining microbial toxins.

Table 38 Processes for storing and preserving beef

Process	Storage life	Chemical change in storage?	Micro-biological change in storage?	Advantages	Disadvantages
None	Less than two days in tropics	Yes	Yes	Cheap	Should be consumed same day as killed
Freezing	1–2 years	Yes	No	Retains its quality	Expensive, needs power
Canning	10 years +	Yes	No	Convenient long-term storage	Needs specialised equipment Eating quality changed
Cooking	Up to 4 days	Yes	Yes	Useful for short-term storage	
Dehydration plus salt (e.g. biltong)	6–12 months	Yes	No	Cheap, can be dried in sun	Acquired taste

Source: adapted from Lawrie (1976)

Appendix
Beef cattle management calendar

Stockowners can maximise the productivity of their beef cattle by forward planning and making decisions and arrangements regarding management of the herd at the correct time. A management calendar provides a useful framework for such planning.

In most parts of Africa, calving can take place throughout the year, although there are peak periods that reflect cow body condition and forage availability at the time of conception (see Chapter 6). Attempts to impose a controlled breeding season should be combined with grazing management and supplementary feeding (if required) to ensure an optimum reproductive rate. Optimum calving rate and growth of calves will be achieved if calves are born shortly before the onset of the rainy season. Milk yield and calf growth respond to the flush of young grass early during the rainy season. The cows gain weight and the probability of re-conception is high; this is especially true in regions with a mean annual rainfall of less than 600 mm. However, in regions of very high rainfall, young calves may be susceptible to infestation with parasites during the wet season.

In high rainfall areas, calves may be born at the end of the rainy season and forage from the main area of range is supplemented by green material (produced in wet areas) and crop residues. Under these conditions, cow body reserves make an important contribution towards the nutrients required for milk production. Normal pre-weaning growth of calves born at this time depends on cows having adequate stored reserves of energy, which in turn depends on plenty of forage being available during the rainy season.

The following calendar has been developed for the summer rainfall (monsoon) areas of southern Africa. For monsoon areas north of the equator the seasons are reversed and the appropriate months are given in brackets.

Month	Calving before rainy season	Calving after end of rainy season
September to November *(Feb to May)*	Check cow herds daily for calving difficulties and retained afterbirths. Number and record new-born calves, dehorn calves before three weeks old. Castrate bull calves before three months. If supplementary protein is given, continue until adequate green grass available. Inoculations: Calves against paratyphoid at 1–3 weeks if this is a problem and against quarter evil at 3 months. Vibriosis (bulls 2 months and cows 1 month before bulling season).	Bulling season: check for inactive bulls. Monitor condition of stock, especially suckling cows, and adjust supplementary feeding as necessary and continue feeding until there is adequate green grass.
December to March *(June to Sept)*	Bulling season: check for inactive bulls (many cows returning to oestrus indicates sub-fertile bulls). Dose all stock over two years old for liver fluke where this is a problem. Dose first calving cows and those in poor condition for round worms.	Wean calves, record weight or condition as an aid to cow selection. Inoculate weaners for quarter evil and heifers – 2nd dose (c. 7 months) for contagious abortion. Dose all stock over two years old for liver fluke if this is a problem.
March to April *(Sept to Oct)*	Assessment of forage supply for dry season must be done now. Estimate herbage density on range and the amounts of crop residues that will be available. Calculate numbers of stock that can be carried. Decide which animals to sell and when. Pregnancy testing at this stage can help this decision. Arrange supply of supplementary forage and concentrates for the dry season.	Same as for pre-rainy season calving.

Month	Calving before rainy season	Calving after end of rainy season
May to June *(Nov to Dec)*	Wean calves, record weight or condition as an aid to cow selection. Start supplementary feeding if animals lose condition (weight). Inoculate weaners against quarter evil and heifer calves (c. 7 months) against contagious abortion.	Check cow herds daily for calving problems. Number and record newborn calves. Dehorn calves before 3 weeks old. Monitor condition of cows and start supplementary feeding as required.
July to September *(Jan to March)*	Monitor condition of stock (especially cows) and adjust supplementary feeding accordingly.	Inoculations: calves for quarter evil at 3 months; vibriosis (bulls 2 months and cows 1 month before bulling season). Dose first calving cows and those in poor condition for round worms.

Glossary

Artificial insemination (AI)   Technique of inserting semen into the female reproductive tract. The term AI is often used to describe the whole process, including dilution and storage of semen

Ad libitum   Providing unrestricted access to feed

Agisting   Practice in which cattle belonging to one owner are cared for by others. In traditional systems, payment is provided by taking milk and some of the calves

Ambient temperature   The temperature of the environment in which the animal is living

Anaemia   Reduction of red blood cells or haemoglobin in the blood

Anaplasmosis (gall sickness)   A rickettsial infection of red blood cells of wild and domestic ruminants with *Anaplasma* spp. Disease is mainly seen in cattle and causes anaemia

Area of rib eye   Cross-sectional area of the muscle (*Longissimus dorsi*), which passes longitudinally through the rib cage

Babesiosis (redwater)   Tick-borne protozoal disease of domestic live-stock caused by *Babesia* spp. that infect red blood cells, causing anaemia and red-coloured urine

Bagasse   Dried fibrous leftovers of sugar cane after sugar has been extracted

Bacteria   Unicellular micro-organisms lacking an organised nucleus. Specialist bacteria ferment the animal's feed in the rumen; diseases are also caused by bacteria

Brucellosis   Bacterial infection of domestic animals caused by one or more of four species of *Brucella*. They infect the reproductive organs and cause abortion

Bush meal   Ground up brushwood and leaves of native woody species that can be used as the basis for survival diets

Campylobacteriosis (vibriosis)   Bacterial venereal infection of cattle caused by *Campylobacter fetus* that results in temporary infertility and occasional abortion

Castration Removing or preventing development of the testes of a bull to control breeding or avoid dark coarse flesh in a mature bull carcass

Catabolism (katabolism) The metabolic process in which complex molecules are broken down into simpler ones with the release of energy

Cattle post (stock post) A cattle post in the Botswana (Southern Africa) context is a livestock watering point (drilled borehole or open well) where cattle are kept. In most cases, where land is communally owned, cattle graze freely or are herded on the range around the cattle post, which is usually the property of an absentee owner and is managed by a few labourers. If the cattle are herded there will be kraals associated with the stock post

Cold carcass weight The weight of the animal after slaughter when the internal organs and the head have been removed

Colostrum The first milk produced by a cow after calving

Compensatory growth The ability of an animal to grow faster after a period of undernutrition than a similar animal of the same age that has been adequately fed throughout its life

Concentrates Highly digestible feeds with high metabolisable energy values (> 10 KJ ME per kg DM); protein concentrates contain more than 250 g crude protein per kg DM

Crossbreeding The mating of animals of different breeds; the progeny are called crossbreds

Crude protein The crude protein content of a feed is obtained by measuring its nitrogen (N) content and multiplying the result by 6.25. The result is expressed as g N per kg DM

Dermatophilosis Bacterial infection of the skin with *Dermatophilus congolensis* causing inflammation of the skin with an oozing serum discharge

Diurnal Happening during the day or daily

Draught The use of cattle for work, either to pull farm implements or for transport

Dry matter (DM) Part of the feed remaining after all the water has been removed

Dystokia Difficulty in calving that requires assistance if the calf is to be born alive and the mother saved, usually associated with calves of above average weight at birth

Effective temperature The likely effect of ambient temperature on the animal body when modified by such factors as wind speed and humidity

Epithelioma A malignant tumour of the epithelial tissue, usually in the skin

Fungi Group of unicellular, multicellular or multinucleate non-photosynthetic organisms that feed on organic matter. Some fungi are involved in the digestion of ligno-cellulose in the rumen, while others may cause diseases such actinomycosis (lumpy jaw) or ringworm

Gross energy   The amount of heat produced by a feed when it is completely burnt; usually measured by combusting the feed in a bomb calorimeter

Heartwater (cowdriosis)   A tick-borne rickettsial infection of ruminants caused by *Cowdria ruminantium* which can cause high fever and death

Heifer   Young female bovine (up to the end of her first lactation)

Heritability   Proportion of phenotypic variation that is due to genetic variation

Heterosis   Extent to which crossbred progeny differ from the average of their parents. Positive heterosis (or hybrid vigour) occurs when the crossbred is better than the average of the parents

Kraaling or corralling   The practice of confining cattle to small enclosures at night to prevent animals on communal grazing from wandering and as protection against predators or theft

Labile body temperature   Body temperature that changes with variations in ambient temperature

Lactation anoestrus   The period when cows are producing significant amounts of milk after calving and do not exhibit oestrus

Laminitis   Inflammation of the sensitive layer, which lies immediately below the outer horny wall of the foot

Legumes   Members of the *Papilionaceae* family; able to convert atmospheric nitrogen into protein with the aid of bacteria in root nodules. They are a valuable source of protein for cattle (e.g. lucerne, desmodium)

Leptospirosis   Disease produced by infection with pathogenic spirochaetes of the genus *Leptospira* that cause fever and jaundice

Lignin   Completely indigestible complex organic polymer deposited in the cell walls of plants, making them rigid and woody

Ligno-cellulose   Physically inseparable mixture of lignin, cellulose and hemi-cellulose; comprises most of the dry matter of roughages

Live weight (or live mass)   Weight of the live animal

Livestock unit (LU)   Animal or group of animals that will eat the same amount of feed as a 450 kg steer gaining 0.5 kg live weight per day; used to assess the effect of different classes of livestock on grazing

Maintenance requirement   Amount of feed (or metabolisable energy) required to keep a non-producing animal at a constant weight

Medulla oblongata   The lower stalk-like section of the brain, continuous with the spinal cord, containing the control centres for the heart and lungs

Metabolic body weight   The live weight of an animal raised to the power 0.75 ($W^{0.75}$). As it grows, the energy requirements for maintenance of an animal increase in line with this figure, not with actual body weight

Metabolisable energy The gross energy of the feed less the losses of energy in the faeces, urine and methane; i.e. the part of the feed energy that can be used by the animal

Molasses Thick, dark syrupy by-product of sugar refining; has a high sugar content; used as an energy source in cattle diets and as a carrier for urea

Nomadism Movement of herds and their human owners over large areas, governed largely by the growth of herbage and availability of water

Oestrus Period of time when a cow will stand to be mated

Off-take The number of cattle removed each year from a herd for slaughter or for sale

Ovulation Shedding of an ovum or ova from the ovary

Oxymyoglobin Pigment formed by the oxidation of myoglobin

Parity Number of parturitions (calvings) recorded by a cow

Pasture In the tropics this term refers to an area of grazing land that has been planted to grasses or a mixture of grasses and legumes

Perinatal Occuring during the period around calving

Plane of nutrition An index of the relative amount of feed given to an animal each day

Postpartum The period of time immediately after birth

Proteolytic enzyme An enzyme that digests protein

Protozoa Unicellular microscopic animals; some species play a role in digestion in the rumen and others cause diseases such as trypano-somiasis and redwater

Puberty The time in the life of an animal when it becomes capable of reproduction. In heifers it means the onset of the first oestrus

Quarter evil Also known as black quarter or blackleg, this is a disease of young grazing cattle (caused by *Clostidium* spp bacterium) that re-sults in lameness and death

Range, rangeland Indigenous vegetation used as grazing and/or brows-ing, which may be composed of a variety of plants

Rift Valley fever Acute infectious virus disease of cattle and sheep trans-mitted by mosquitoes or midges

Roughage Animal feed that has more than 150 g fibre per kg dry matter

Sedentary animal production The herds and flocks remain at one site all the year and the owners live in settled accommodation

Steer Castrated bull

Stocking rate Density of animals in a grazing area, expressed as the number (or fraction) of head or animal units per hectare

Stratification Integrated use of various climatic zones for different forms of animal production (e.g. cattle rearing in semi-arid zones and beef fattening in high rainfall areas)

Theileriosis   Tick-borne protozoal infections of domestic ruminants caused by *Theileria* spp. One such disease is East Coast fever

Thermoregulation   Method by which an animal maintains a constant body temperature

Toxicosis   The symptoms caused by the presence of toxin(s) in the blood, e.g. from bacterial infection

Transhumance   Seasonal movement of herds and flocks, related to seasonal rainfall and taking advantage of available herbage; may be associated with settled habitation with only certain members of the family tending the animals

Trichomonosis   Venereal protozoal infection of cattle caused by *Trichomonas* that can cause abortion

Tropical livestock unit (TLU)   Animal or group of animals that will eat the same amount of feed as a 250 kg bovine

Trypanosomiasis   Disease caused by protozoan parasites of the genus *Trypanosoma* and transmitted by tsetse flies

Trypanotolerant   Animals that can resist the effects of *Trypanosoma* infection

Venereal disease   Disease transmitted during mating (e.g. brucellosis or vibriosis)

Vleis   Also known as *dhambos* (Zambia and Malawi), *mbuga* (Tanzania) and *fadama* (Nigeria); areas that are waterlogged in the wet season and in which the water table is 50 to 100 cm below the surface in the dry season. Herbage growth occurs in the dry season using residual soil moisture

Volatile fatty acids   End products of digestion of carbohydrates in the rumen, comprising acetic, propionic, butyric and valeric acids. They are volatile at 100°C and may be collected by steam distillation

$W^{0.75}$ Denotes metabolic body weight or weight to the power three quarters. The rate of metabolism in the body increases as the animal grows in line with this measurement and not in line with actual body weight

Weaning   The end of the period during which calves consume milk

Weight stasis   Maintaining a more or less constant body weight

Bibliography

Agricultural and Food Research Council (AFRC) Technical Committee on Responses to Nutrients (1993) Energy and Protein Requirements of Ruminants. CAB International: Wallingford, UK.

Agyemang, K. (1992) Adjustment of birth weight for weighing age and relationship of standardised birth weight with early mortality in N'Dama calves under traditional husbandry systems in the Gambia. *Animal Production* 55: 301–308.

Baker, P.R. (1981) *Sociological Implications of Encouraging Intensive Animal Production in Developing Countries: the case of the animal pastoralists.* British Society of Animal Production: Thames Ditton, UK.

Bayer, W. and A. Walters-Bayer (1998) *Forage Husbandry.* The Tropical Agriculturalist. Macmillan: London and Basingstoke, UK.

Behnke, R.H., I. Scoones and C. Kerven (1993) *Range Ecology at Disequilibrium.* Overseas Development Institute: London, UK.

Bekure, S., P.N. de Leeuw, B.E. Grandin and P.J.H. Neate (1991) Analysis of the livestock production system of Maasai pastoralists in eastern Kajiado District, Kenya. International Livestock Centre for Africa: Addis Ababa, Ethiopia.

Bembridge, T.J. and D. Tapson (1993) Communal Livestock Systems. In: Maree, C. and N.H. Casey (eds.) *Livestock Production Systems.* Agri-Development Foundation: Brooklyn, South Africa.

Blair-Rains, A. and A.H. Kassim (1979) Land resources and animal production. Working paper No. 8. FAO/UNFPA project INT/75/P13. Food and Agriculture Organization of the United Nations: Rome, Italy.

Butterworth, M.H. (1985) *Beef Cattle Nutrition and Tropical Pastures.* Longman: London, UK.

Chesworth, J. (1992) *Ruminant Nutrition.* The Tropical Agriculturalist. Macmillan: London and Basingstoke, UK.

Colditz, P.J. and R.C. Kellaway (1972) The effect of diet and heat stress on feed intake, growth and nitrogen metabolism in Friesian, F_1

Brahman x Friesian and Brahman heifers. *Australian Journal of Agricultural Research* 23: 717–725.

de Castro, J.J. (1991) Resistance to Ixodid ticks in cattle with an assessment of its role in tick control in Africa. In: Owen, J.B. and R.F.E. Axford (eds.) *Breeding for Disease Resistance in Farm Animals.* CAB International: Wallingford, UK.

Dye, P.J. and P.T. Spear (1982) The effects of bush clearing and rainfall variability on grass yield and composition in south-west Zimbabwe. *Zimbabwe Journal of Agricultural Research* 20: 103–118.

Elliott, R.C. (1967) Voluntary intake of low protein diets by ruminants. *Journal of Agricultural Science, Cambridge* 69: 375–382.

Elliott, R.C. and W.D.C. Reed (1968) Studies of high concentrates for cattle: Growth and food intake of steers fed on diets containing different levels of low-quality roughage. *South African Journal of Agricultural Science* 11: 713–722.

Elliott, R.C., K. Fokkema, and C.H. French (1961) Herbage consumption studies on beef cattle: Intake studies on Afrikander and Mashona cows on veld grazing (1959–60). *Rhodesia Agricultural Journal* 58: 124–130.

Elliott, R.C., W.R. Mills and W.D.C. Reed (1966) Survival feeding of Africander cows. *Rhodesia, Zambia and Malawi Journal of Agricultural Research* 4: 69–75.

FAO (2004) Statistical Databases. Food and Agriculture Organization of the United Nations http://apps.fao.org/page/collections?subset=agriculture

Forse, B. (1999) *Where There is No Vet.* Macmillan: Oxford and London, UK.

Frisch, J.E. (1981) Changes occurring in cattle as a result of selection for growth rate in a stressful environment. *Journal of Agricultural Science, Cambridge* 96: 23–38.

Frisch, J.E. and J.E. Vercoe (1984) An analysis of different cattle genotypes reared in different environments. *Journal of Agricultural Science, Cambridge* 103: 137–153.

Gemeda, T., E. Zerbini, A.G. Wold and D. Demisse (1995) Effect of draught work on performance and metabolism of crossbred cows: Effect of work and diet on body-weight change, body condition, lactation and productivity. *Animal Science* 60: 361–367.

Grant, J.L. (1977) Effects of feeding in early summer, late summer and/or in winter. Annual Report (1975–76), Division of Livestock and Pastures. Department of Research and Specialist Services: Salisbury, Rhodesia.

Groenewald, I.B. and J.D.H. Hopley (1976) Steers fattened with diets containing either maize or molasses as sources of energy. Annual Report (1974–75), Division of Livestock and Pastures. Department of Research and Specialist Services: Salisbury, Rhodesia.

Herd, R.M. (1995). Effect of divergent selection for yearling growth rate on the maintenance feed requirements of mature Angus cows. *Livestock Production Science* 41: 39–49.

Hodgson, J. and A.W. Illius (1996) *The Ecology and Management of Grazing Systems*. CAB International: Wallingford, UK.

Holness, D.H., D.H. Hale and J.D.H. Hopley (1980). Ovarian activity and conception during the post-partum period in Afrikaner and Mashona cows. *Zimbabwe Journal of Agricultural Research* 18: 2–11.

Holness, D.H. (1991). *Pigs*. The Tropical Agriculturalist. Macmillan: London and Basingstoke, UK.

Hunter, A. (1994) *Animal Health Volume 2 (Specific Diseases)*. The Tropical Agriculturalist. Macmillan: London and Basingstoke, UK.

Hunter, A. (1996) *Animal Health Volume 1 (General Principles)*. The Tropical Agriculturalist. Macmillan: London and Basingstoke, UK.

Hunter, R.A. and T. Magner (1990) Effect of trenbolone acetate on urea metabolism in cattle fed low-protein roughage diets. *Journal of Agricultural Science, Cambridge* 114: 55–58.

Hunter, R.A. and B.D. Siebert (1985) Utilization of low-quality hay by *Bos taurus* and *Bos indicus* cattle. 1. Rumen digestion. *British Journal of Nutrition* 53: 637–648.

Jasiorowski, H.A. (1976) The developing world as a source of beef for world markets. In: Smith, A.J. (ed.) *Beef Cattle Production in Developing Countries*. Centre for Tropical Veterinary Medicine, University of Edinburgh: Edinburgh, UK.

Lawrie, R.A. (1976) Problems of beef quality in relation to transportation, slaughter and storage. In: Smith, A.J. (ed.) *Beef Cattle Production in Developing Countries*. Centre for Tropical Veterinary Medicine, University of Edinburgh: Edinburgh, UK.

Ledger, H.P. and A.R. Sayers (1977) The utilization of dietary energy by steers during periods of restricted food intake and subsequent realimentation. *Journal of Agricultural Science, Cambridge* 88: 11–33.

Manteca, X. and A.J. Smith (2004) *Livestock Behaviour, Management and Welfare*. The Tropical Agriculturalist. Macmillan: Oxford, UK.

Mason, I.L. (1996) *A World Dictionary of Livestock Breeds, Types and Varieties* (4th edition). CAB International: Wallingford, UK.

Maule, J.P. (1990) *The Cattle of the Tropics*. Centre for Tropical Veterinary Medicine, University of Edinburgh: Edinburgh, UK.

Mezzadra, C., J. Escuder and M.C. Miquiel (1992) Effects of genotype and stocking density on post-weaning daily gain and meat production per hectare in cattle. *Animal Production* 55: 65–72.

Nicholson, M.J. (1987) The effect of drinking frequency on some aspects of the productivity of Zebu cattle. *Journal of Agricultural Science, Cambridge* 108: 119–128.

Nicholson, S.E. (2001) Climatic and environmental change in Africa during the last two centuries. *Climatic Research* 17: 123–144.

Osborn, D.F. (1976) The utilisation of natural grasslands in the tropics. In: Smith, A.J. (ed.) *Beef Cattle Production in Developing Countries.* Centre for Tropical Veterinary Medicine, University of Edinburgh: Edinburgh, UK.

Pagot, J. (1985) *L'Elevage en Pays Tropicaux.* Maisonneuve et Larose: Paris, France.

Parks, J.R. (1982) A Theory of Feeding and Growth of Animals. Springer-Verlag: Berlin, Germany.

Payne, W.J.A. and J. Hodges (1997) *Tropical Cattle Origins, Breeds and Breeding Policies.* Blackwell Science: Oxford, UK.

Payne, W.J.A. and R.T. Wilson (1999) *An Introduction to Animal Husbandry in the Tropics.* Blackwell Science: Oxford, UK.

Pullen, N.P. (1978) Condition scoring of Fulani cattle. *Tropical Animal Health and Production* 10(2): 118–120.

Pratt, D.J. (2005) Notes on some problems in the assessment of livestock carrying capacity. Food and Agriculture Organization of the United Nations: http://www.fao.org/wairdocs/ilri/x5543b/x5543b12.htm

Richardson, F.D. (1983) The short- and long-term influences of undernutrition on range cattle production. *Zimbabwe Agricultural Journal* 80: 175–182.

Richardson, F.D. and R.V. Khaka (1981) Stocking rate and the provision of different amounts of protein rich concentrates to cattle grazing on veld. Annual Report (1979–80). Division of Livestock and Pastures, Department of Research and Specialist Services: Harare, Zimbabwe.

Richardson, F.D. and R.V. Khaka (1983) Stocking rate and the provision of different amounts of protein rich concentrates to cattle grazing on veld. Annual Report (1981–82). Division of Livestock and Pastures, Department of Research and Specialist Services: Harare, Zimbabwe.

Richardson, F.D. and J.W. Thomson (1984). The growth of heifers and their concepta. *Zimbabwe Journal of Agricultural Research* 22: 1–14.

Richardson, F.D., J. Oliver and G.P.Y. Clark (1979) Analyses of some factors that affect the productivity of beef cows and their calves in a marginal rainfall area of Rhodesia. 3. Factors affecting calf birth weight, growth to 240 days and the use of concentrates by cows and their calves. *Animal Production* 28: 199–222.

Richardson, F.D., B.D. Hahn and S.J. Schoeman (2000) Modelling nutrient utilization in livestock grazing semi-arid rangeland. In: McNamara, J.P., J. France and D.E. Beever (eds.) *Modelling Nutrient Utilization in Farm Animals.* CAB International: Wallingford, UK.

Robertshaw, D. and V. Finch (1976) The effects of climate on the productivity of beef cattle. In: Smith, A.J. (ed.) *Beef Cattle Production in Developing Countries.* Centre for Tropical Veterinary Medicine, University of Edinburgh: Edinburgh, UK.

Roder, R. (1992) Survival and development: Household strategies of the Sahel's 'New Pastoralists'. MSc Thesis, Centre of African Studies, University of Edinburgh: Edinburgh, UK.

Ryan, W.J., A.H. Williams and R.J. Moir (1993) Compensatory growth in sheep and cattle: Changes in body composition and tissue weights. *Australian Journal of Agricultural Research* 44: 1623–1633.

Schaefer-Kehnert, W. (1981) Appraisal and finance of intensive animal production schemes. In: Smith, A.J. and G.R. Gunn (eds.) *Intensive Animal Production in Developing Countries*. British Society of Animal Production: Edinburgh, UK.

Schimdt, M.I. (1990) The Relation between Cattle and Savings. Development Research, AGRICOR: Mmabatho, South Africa.

Scoones, I. (1993) Why are there so many animals? Cattle population dynamics in the communal areas of Zimbabwe. In: Behnke, R.H., I. Scoones and C. Kerven (eds.) *Range Ecology at Disequilibrium*. Overseas Development Institute: London, UK.

Scoones, I. (1995) Exploiting heterogeneity: habitat use by cattle in dryland Zimbabwe. *Journal of Arid Environments* 29: 221–237.

Simpson, M.C. (1980) *Sector Appraisal Manual: Beef*. Overseas Development Administration: London, UK.

Smith, A.J. (ed.) (1976) *Beef Cattle Production in Developing Countries*. Centre for Tropical Veterinary Medicine, University of Edinburgh: Edinburgh, UK.

Smith, A.J. (1981) Concluding remarks. In: Smith, A.J. and R.G. Gunn (eds.) *Intensive Animal Production in Developing Countries*. British Society of Animal Production: Thames Ditton, UK.

Stobbs, T.H. (1973a) The effect of plant structure on the intake of tropical pastures: Variation in the bite size of grazing cattle. *Australian Journal of Agricultural Research* 24: 809–819.

Stobbs, T.H. (1973b) Beef production from sown and planted pastures in the tropics. In: Smith, A.J. (ed.) *Beef Cattle Production in Developing Countries*. Centre for Tropical Veterinary Medicine, University of Edinburgh: Edinburgh, UK.

Tainton, N.M. (1999) *Veld Management in South Africa*. University of Natal Press: Pietermaritzburg, South Africa.

Tapson, D. (1993). Biological sustainability in pastoral systems: The Kwazulu case. In: Behnke, R.H., I. Scoones and C. Kerven (eds.) *Range Ecology at Disequilibrium*. Overseas Development Institute: London, UK.

Tawonezvi, H.P., H.K. Ward, J.C.M. Trail and D. Light (1988a) Evaluation of beef breeds for rangeland weaner production in Zimbabwe. 1 Productivity of purebred cows. *Animal Production* 47: 351–359.

Tawonezvi, H.P., H.K. Ward, J.C.M. Trail and D. Light (1988b) Evaluation of beef breeds for rangeland weaner production in Zimbabwe.

2 Productivity of crossbred cows and heterosis estimates. *Animal Production* 47: 361–367.

Trail, J.C.M., N.G. Buck, D. Light, T.W. Rennie, A. Rutherford, M. Miller, D. Pratchett and B.S. Capper (1977) Productivity of Africander, Tswana, Tuli and crossbred cattle in Botswana. *Animal Production* 24: 57—62.

Ward, H.K. (1968) Supplementation of beef cows grazing on veld. *Rhodesian Journal of Agricultural Research* 6: 93–101.

Ward, H.K. and T.S. Clark (1984). Selection Responses and Genotype x Environment Interaction in Beef Cattle. Annual Report (1981—82), Division of Livestock and Pastures, Department of Research and Specialist Services: Harare, Zimbabwe.

Ward, H.K., J. Davidson, A. Prentice, J de W. Tiffin, J.W.I. Brownlee, H.R. Harvey, S.P. Arrowsmith, S. Bennett, J.N. Sarai, I. Dube and G. Moyo (1978). Improvement of beef cattle through crossbreeding. Annual Report, 1976–77, Division of Livestock and Pastures, Department of Research and Specialist Services: Salisbury, Rhodesia.

Weiner, G. (1994) *Animal Breeding*. The Tropical Agriculturalist. Macmillan: London and Basingstoke, UK.

Index

Note: page numbers in italics refer to figures, tables or illustrations. Glossary entries are in bold.

117